A Walk IN THE City

AN INCOMPLETE TOUR

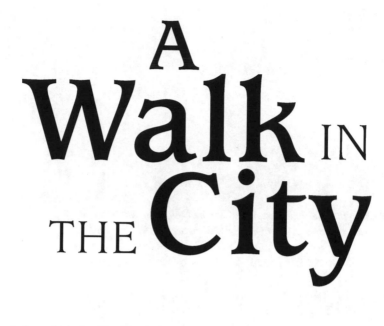

Thomas Porky McDonald

authorHOUSE®

AuthorHouse™
1663 Liberty Drive
Bloomington, IN 47403
www.authorhouse.com
Phone: 1-800-839-8640

Published by AuthorHouse   12/16/2014

ISBN: 978-1-4-9695-937-9 (sc)
ISBN: 978-1-4969-5938-6 (e)

Other books by Thomas Porky McDonald:

An Irishman's Tribute to the Negro Leagues

Over the Shoulder and Plant on One:
An Irishman's Tribute to Willie Mays

Where the Angels Bow to the Grass: A Boy's Memoir

The Air That September

Hit Sign, Win Suit: An Irishman's Tribute to Ebbets Field

Series Endings: A Whimsical Look at the Final Plays
of Baseball's Fall Classic, 1903-2003

At a Loss to Eternity:
Baseball Teams of Note That Didn't Win it All

Never These Men: One Man's Look at Baseball's
Creatively Cultured Characters

Does the Toy Cannon Fire Still at Night?

the skipper's scrapbook

Poet in the Grandstand: An Enlightened Tour of Ballparks
and the Places Where They Live: 1990-2010

Poetry Collections

Ground Pork: Poems 1989-1994
Downtown Revival: Poems 1994-1997
Closer to Rona: Poems 1997-1999
Diamond Reflections: Baseball Pieces For Real Fans
Dem Poems: The Brooklyn Collection
Still Chuckin': Poems 1999-2002
In the Cameo Shade: Poems 2002-2005
Vespers at Sunset: Poems 2005-2007

Short Stories

Paradise Oval..and other Tallman Tales

Jacket Design and Formatting
by Olga Khrapovitski

Covers Photos of Empire State Building, MCU
Park, Hall of Science Rocket Park & NYC Fire
Museum exhibit by Lance Tallman

Edited by Paula Alleyne, Asya Muid,
Olga Khrapovitski & Lisa Schwartz

Acknowledgements

I'd like to thank my good friends and longtime co-workers Asya Muid, Paula Alleyne and Olga Khrapovitski, who suggested my name to Lisa Schwartz, who was looking for some baseball pieces for the *MTA Today* webpage in 2012. I am also very grateful to Lisa and her colleagues, Gene Ribeiro, Ann Steimel and Connie DePalma, who encouraged me to continue writing travel-related pieces for the site, which essentially created all the work in this book. Moreover, they have always given my work a free reign and have been receptive to anything that I submitted to them. The best part about working in a place like NYC Transit is the people and those just mentioned certainly exemplify that notion. I am also grateful for all the positive input that I received as my pieces began to appear on *MTA Today* on a fairly regular basis, especially from my friends/co-workers Andy Bata, Anjali Mahashabde, Rosemary Magee, Terry Glynn, Pat Morrison, Arthur Mahler, Suzanne Michelle, Chaim Kupferstein, Gary Dwyer and Bill Beren and fellow Transit workers Priscilla Lindsay-Sullivan, Patrice Norwood, Joe Kalmanowitz and Krishna Kashyap. Special thanks to my friend/co-worker Diane Castellano, who turned me onto the Morris-Jumel Mansion and transit workers Michael Cartuongo, Joe Primo and Francine Menaker, who pointed out typos and/or oversights which have been cleared up in this book. Thanks to all my baseball people, particularly Don Phu, Janice Joe and Arnold Greene, who went to the MLB FanFest at the Javits Center with me in 2013 and my road trip partner, Adam Boneker. And lastly to my special friend Monah Johnson, who walked the completed High Line with me, joined me at Schomburg Center and came along on a very wonderful Sunday when we went with our friend and co-worker, Frank Rosa and his lovely daughter, Gigi, to the American Museum of Natural History.

This Book
is Dedicated to
all those who walk
through the streets
of New York City,
in search of something
they're not quite sure of,
yet know it intimately,
each and every time
they come upon it.

AND TO:

All the Members of
St. Joseph's School
Class of 1975
40 years later, yet still an inspiration
Forward, my Friends!!

In Memoriam

**Marie Everding McDonald
(1929-2014)**

Here's where I went today, mom

Contents

A Walk in the City

Took a walk in the City,
just a walk in the City;
Not a jog or a jaunt,
but a walk in the City;
And it's cold never early,
though the wind shifts to swirly;
But the walk is eventful,
for the meek or the burly.

They don't talk in the City,
they just walk in the City;
Even drivers, bikers, runners,
they all walk in the City;
All the cops and the hookers
scan the sights and the lookers;
They all walk right beside me
in this mad pressure cooker.

As I walk in the City
and I jot down this ditty,
I'm fulfilled and amazed
on my walk in the City;
There's a guy I just filed
singing *"Born to be Wild;"*
Though it seems on my birthday
all these loud streets are mild.

So I walk in the City,
where the sights aren't all pretty;
But it's home and its mine,
so I walk in the City;
So we walk in the City;
Push the nitty to the gritty;
You can't run from your heartbeat;
You can walk in the City.

A Brief Introduction

Exercises in Economy

In the Summer of 2012, the *MTA Today*, an internal website homepage, decided to run a series on New York City baseball. I was asked to write a few pieces for this series by Lisa Schwartz of Corporate Communications, which gathers and runs the contents of the page. She had previously used my work on two occasions, one a profile of my book, *Poet in the Grandstand*, for a series they ran on writers in Transit and the other about the recently opened *9/11 Memorial*. For the baseball articles, Lisa had been sent my way by three good friends who are webmasters for MTA New York City Transit, Paula Alleyne, Olga Khrapovitski and Asya Muid. I was asked that each profile not exceed 450 words. To be honest, at first I felt this limitation afforded me a very small window to write about the things that I wanted to cover. In any case, I turned in four pieces, on Citi Field, the new Yankee Stadium, the Brooklyn Cyclones and a remembrance of Shea Stadium and the World's Fair of 1964. My work was well received by Lisa and her department, so much so that they asked me if I could write more articles, about other New York-themed items. After kicking it around a bit, I agreed to do what were essentially mini-travelogues. The only prerequisites I was given were the original 450-word limit and that the final paragraph would give the reader directions to the particular site, via transit buses or trains. So off I went.

One of the old adages that lifetime New Yorkers (like me) grow up hearing and later sharing is that so many of us don't go to see many of the great places that *The City* has to offer, even though we live here. This is true, to varying degrees, as I know New Yorkers who have never even been to the Empire State Building, the Statue of Liberty or the Brooklyn Bridge, three places you simply *HAVE to* go to if you are from New York City, in my opinion. This *MTA Today* assignment gave me the chance to explore New York City (which I had always walked the streets of throughout my life) in a much deeper way than I previously had done. I had long ago decided that by the time I retired, I would visit as many small and large New York sites as I could. Lisa Schwartz and the good folks at the *MTA Today*, notably Gene Ribeiro, Ann Steimel and Connie DePalma, the others who accepted my work, had escalated my timetable and given me a rare gift, one I would gratefully take advantage of. The one item that concerned me at first had been the 450-word limit. But as I began visiting different places and then writing the pieces about them, I found myself embracing the limit and using it as a great way to try and put the most information possible into the least possible words. These exercises in economy became an absolute joy and something I was very happy to share.

At some point, I realized that these mini-travelogues could make a nice book. The title was easy enough to figure out, as I had quickly looked up a poem I had written many years earlier, one that I somehow knew I would use one day. A piece I wrote on my 36th birthday called *"A Walk in the City,"* seemed perfect for this project, even though the nature of the pieces that *MTA Today* requested was to give you the way around town by bus or subway. But I've always held that to truly appreciate *The City* (which meant Manhattan, of course), one needed to utilize the subways and city buses as merely a tool to hit the streets running (or walking, in this case). So to further justify this book's title, I have added a "Walking Distance" add-on after each piece, as to what else is near a particular venue. For arguments sake, my idea of walking distance is about 10 city blocks or 4 avenues; that is the criteria I used here. Naturally, there is a fair amount of cross-sectioning that goes on, but I hope that the choice of going to a certain place might spread to other nearby attractions and/ or curiosities, after reading each connecting list. While most of the pieces are based in Manhattan, outer boroughs are also represented.

What follows are some 70 pieces that I wrote, which were then posted on the *MTA Today* homepage on the days noted at the end of each piece. The pieces are almost all presented exactly as they were printed on *MTA Today*, though on a few there have been minor small edits made. Some of the earlier pieces I wrote, particularly the museum spots, spoke in real time, as to what was appearing at a particular site at the time, or what I did while visiting there. One could accurately call them dated material, but I chose to balance the integrity of the original pieces with giving the reader what a trip to a particular place *would feel like*. Telling you about an exhibit that is long gone by now may seem useless to the reader, but I wanted to maintain how the original piece looked. The spirit of adventure at what might be showing now has to enter into the equation for these pieces. Also, most of the museum websites offer a "previous exhibits" area, where some of those that I saw are still alive, albeit electronically. (I even mention an exhibit I'd seen years before that is now on the website of the *Museum of the City of New York*.) Moreover, where my by-line originally was is replaced herein by the website of the venue, or an otherwise relevant website. For instance, on the piece on remembering Shea Stadium and the 1964-65 World's Fair, I list the World's Fair historical website. For the piece about the Cirque du Soleil show that I saw in a makeshift tent in the Citi Field parking lot, I use the Cirque's website, so that one can see when the various new shows return to Citi Field or Radio City Music Hall, the two usual venues that the Cirque uses in this area. The piece on the pre-2013 All-Star Game *MLB FanFest*, which I went to with my baseball friends/Transit co-workers Arnold Greene, Janice Joe and Don Phu, uses the Javits Center website, the place where the *FanFest* was held. All the websites listed were active at the time this book was published.

The first section of the book covers various attractions in *The City* and the second section contains a pack of large and small museums. Profiles of books and book collections of mine that appeared on the *MTA Today* are in the third section and the final piece in the book is one I wrote about how Transit workers reconnected following Hurricane Sandy, which allowed me to close the book by citing the official MTA website, a most fitting ending, I'd say.

The subtitle of this book states *"An Incomplete Tour"* and that is about as sincere as I can be. It wasn't my intention to write about every possible place in New York that one might see. The pieces here are neither comprehensive nor overbearing, as I have seen in many travel books. They are merely brief vignettes, ones that I hope will spur the readers' imagination, to go out and see some of the more famous sites as well as the hidden jewels. I can imagine a second volume of these pieces in the future, but let's not get ahead of ourselves; there will always be other things to see in the most interesting city on Earth.

Until that time, walk on.

T.P. McDonald
On the Southern Tip of Manhattan
10/22/14

Note: I organized the Table of Contents alphabetically, by the title I had given each piece. One will note that I don't subscribe to standard rules of alphabetizing. I don't put an "A" or a "The" after a comma at the end of a title. This is particularly relevant to me in that some museums use the word "The" in the museum's official title, while others don't choose to be as declarative.

(1)

Baseball, Icons & Other Activities

A Trip to Citi Field

http://newyork.mets.mlb.com/nym/ballpark/information/
index.jsp

For those of us who grew up going to Met games at Shea Stadium, there was nothing like looking out the window of the Elevated #7 Flushing line as it pulled out of the 111th Street station. Within a few moments, the huge ballpark rose up above the trees, like a Colossus, as you neared the *Willets Point-Shea Stadium* station. Whether the Mets won or not, that first look at Shea was a thrill so many treasured, one which passed on in the Winter of 2008. Since April of 2009, Citi Field has evolved, if not as a replacement for Shea, but as an arena fully representative of the *Age of New Ballparks*, which began with the opening of Camden Yards in Baltimore in 1992. Now in its fourth year of existence, Citi has settled in as a fine local yard, with its' classic Ebbets Field themed front entrance, the historically significant *Jackie Robinson Rotunda* and one of the widest varieties of ballpark food in the Majors. I don't think it will ever be the same as Shea to those of us who grew up in the 60's and 70's, but it is an appreciated home field, at least from where I'm sitting.

In the first three seasons as the new home of the Mets, Citi Field eased its way into the consciousness with wonderful sight lines in both the upper and lower levels. For kids coming to Citi, there is a fantastic area beyond the scoreboard in centerfield, where they can play wiffle ball in a mini-stadium, hit in small batting cages, play video games or try and drop an obnoxious worker sitting on a platform at a waterless dunk tank. As previously noted, there is an astonishing variety of foods at Citi. As someone who has gone to parks all over the country, I'd say Citi's menu, which includes burgers, dogs, fish, chicken, tacos and pizza, is right up there with those found in the new parks in San Francisco, Minnesota and Milwaukee, three that I would rate as the best places to eat in the Majors. The fabulous *Jackie Robinson Rotunda* and the adjoining *Mets Hall of Fame*, could enlighten even the most alien newcomer to the ballpark experience. The Mets, as the caretaker of a great legacy, that of New York National League baseball, are the only team who could credibly honor the most important event in American sports history, the signing of Jackie Robinson in Brooklyn, 1947.

These days, if you get up as the El train pulls out of 111th Street, you may no longer see a large park rising from the trees, but just to the East, old timers will glimpse something resembling their dear, old Ebbets Field, while youngsters can envision a park they can call their own.

- *MTA Today, New York City Transit Edition, 6/22/12*

<u>**Walking Distance**</u>: Flushing Meadows-Corona Park, USTA Billie Jean King National Tennis Center; Queens Museum, Queens Zoo, New York Hall of Science, Main Street shopping district.

A Walk on the Brooklyn Bridge

http://www.nyc.gov/html/dot/html/infrastructure/brooklyn-bridge.shtml

The most iconic bridge in the world took 14 years to complete, but in the past 129 years it has become a statement for honoring and preserving things done correctly. In today's world where something new is embraced by so many as superior, often despite evidence to the contrary, the *Brooklyn Bridge* reminds us that true greatness was around long before any of us were born. You have every right to spend absurd amounts on a new telephone-based gadget every six months if you like, but if you want the finest view of the Manhattan skyline (while keeping your feet on the ground), a walk across the *Brooklyn Bridge* is the only answer. All for free.

John A. Roebling began building the most adventurous bridge of his time in 1869, a few years after completing a smaller, similar structure across the Ohio River, which linked Cincinnati, Ohio and Covington, Kentucky. When Roebling died of tetanus soon after construction began, the result of his foot being crushed in an on-site accident, his 32-year old son Washington took over the project. A phenomenon that the construction of the *Brooklyn Bridge* offered was the so-called caisson disease (or "the bends") which afflicted many of those who worked beneath the water inside one of the two large pneumatic caissons, where workers anchored the bridge. Washington Roebling himself suffered from this malady and spent the final years of the project watching the site from a window in a room on the Brooklyn side, while his very capable wife, Emily, took over the day-to-day operations. The final structure, featuring two quickly familiar arched towers and crisscrossing "steel ropes" that formed a look which has delighted poets, writers and artists to this day, opened to the public on May 24, 1883.

At various times, horse-drawn carriages, trolleys, elevated trains and streetcars passed over the bridge. Today, there are six lanes of automobile traffic and a bike lane on the bridge (utilized by countless many), but walking is a still the best way to cross the Brooklyn

Bridge and a must for anyone who aspires to explore one of New York City's greatest landmarks. Whichever direction you choose to walk it, the Brooklyn Bridge offers the finest view of the Manhattan skyline and the Downtown areas of both *The City* and the Borough of Churches.

The Brooklyn Bridge can be accessed on the Manhattan side, by taking the 4 or the 5 train to the *Brooklyn Bridge-City Hall* stop, or the R train to the *City Hall* stop. Both these stations leave you right at the tip of the bridge. On the Brooklyn side, you can take the 2, 3, 4, 5 or R trains to the *Court Street-Borough Hall* station, which leaves you just a short walk from the bridge.

- ***MTA Today, New York City Transit Edition, 10/12/12***

Walking Distance: *Brooklyn*: DUMBO; Brooklyn Promenade; Brooklyn Historical Society; NYC Transit Museum; Fulton Street Mall; Metrotech Business Improvement District; *Manhattan*: City Hall Park; The Anne Frank Center USA; 9/11 Memorial and Museum; Trinity Church; The New York City Police Museum; Canyon of Heroes.

Alexander Hamilton Gravesite
(in the Trinity Church Courtyard)

http://www.trinitywallstreet.org

For all those who work in the Financial District in Downtown Manhattan, there is a unique historical site which many people are not even aware of, located within another landmark venue which took on even more significance, following a recent, tragic world event.

Alexander Hamilton, one of the most important figures in United States' history, is best known as the man who created the American financial system still in place today. He is also famous for the way he died, in an 1804 duel with then U.S. Vice President Aaron Burr. His gravesite, located in the *Trinity Church Courtyard*, has seen recent renovations completed and can now once again be visited by the general public.

Trinity Church, located at 79 Broadway, is the third house of worship so named in the area of Downtown Manhattan. It was opened in 1846, replacing *Trinity #2*, which was torn down after severe snow storms in the winter of 1838-39 damaged its infrastructure. The *Original Trinity Church*, constructed in 1698, burned down during the Great Fire of New York, which started on September 21, 1776, in the early days of the British occupation of *The City* during the American Revolutionary War. *Trinity Church* was one of over 500 buildings to burn down in the fire. The second *Trinity Church* began construction in 1788 and was completed in 1790.

The current structure's 284-foot high spire and cross claimed the highest point in New York City upon completion in 1846, until being surpassed in 1890 by the *New York World Building* (also known as the *Pulitzer Building*), which was demolished in 1955. *Trinity Church*, which had been given New York City landmark status in 1966 and been designated a National Historic Landmark in 1976, became famous once again in September of 2001, as a staging area for the wounded in and around the World Trade Center, following the terrorist attacks of 9/11.

The *Trinity Church Courtyard*, adjacent to the church, is a burial grounds for a number of historical individuals, the most famous being engineer and inventor Robert Fulton and of course, Alexander Hamilton, the 1st United States Secretary of Treasury, under George Washington. The placement of his tomb just south of Wall Street and the financial district seems appropriate to many. The church, the courtyard and Hamilton's tomb are open daily, for tourists or local workers on their lunch break to pass through, pray and/or reflect upon.

The 2, 3, 4 and 5 trains to Wall Street leave you right near the *Trinity Church Courtyard*. The 1 and R trains to Rector Street leave you at the rear end of the courtyard.

- ***MTA Today, New York City Transit Edition, 7/8/14***

Walking Distance: Wall Street/New York Stock Exchange; The New York City Police Museum; 9/11 Memorial and Museum; National Museum of the American Indian/New York; Museum of Jewish Heritage; Skyscraper Museum; Fraunces Tavern; Canyon of Heroes.

Apollo Theater

https://www.apollotheater.org

One of the most famous entertainment venues the world over still stands in its uptown Manhattan home. The *Apollo Theater*, located at 125th Street off Frederick Douglass Boulevard in Harlem, remains a most vibrant part of that community, with a history of unprecedented acts which have performed there fueling the continuing quest to deliver new talent yet to come.

Originally a burlesque theater designed by George Keister and initially owned by Sidney Cohen, the theater, constructed in 1914, was called *Hurtig & Seamon's New Burlesque Theater*, after Benjamin Hurtig and Harry Seamon secured a long term lease on the property. In those days, African-Americans were not allowed as paying customers or to perform there, an irony that would resonate in the coming decades. In the 1930's, New York Mayor Fiorello LaGuardia, in one of his dogged campaigns, closed many burlesque houses, including *Hurtig & Seamon's*. Cohen returned with a partner, Morris Sussman, to re-open the site as the *Apollo Theater* in 1934, with the emphasis on variety revues. The marketing of the venue was also shifted toward the growing African-American community in Harlem.

In its heyday, from the 1930's through the 1950's, the *Apollo* was the most sought out hall to play for the great entertainers of the day, such as Duke Ellington, Cab Calloway, Billie Holiday and Ella Fitzgerald. The emergence of the Motown sound in the 1960's infused the *Apollo* with a fresh batch of hit makers, as headliners like the Supremes, the Four Tops, the Temptations and countless others all took their turns playing there. Frank Schiffman and Leo Brecher ran the *Apollo* from 1935 until the late 1970's, when the fabled hall almost closed down for good. In 1981, Percy Sutton and a group of investors bought the *Apollo* and refurbished it, including a recording and television studio, which has served the theater well into the 21st Century.

The *Apollo*, now surrounded by a slew of new businesses that underscore the historical significance of the theater, continues to deliver quality entertainment. *"Amateur Night,"* a staple at the *Apollo* for decades, carries on in various forms and specialty shows like veteran entertainer Maurice Hines' *"Apollo Club Harlem"* revue make the *Apollo Theater* another must-see for New Yorkers and world travelers alike. Known for audiences which often interact with the performers on stage, the *Apollo Theater*, a most intimate hall whose walls drip with the history of American music, is a treasure, one which received city and state landmark status in 1983.

If you *"Take the "A" Train,"* or the B, C, D, 1, 2 or 3 trains, to their 125th Street stations, you will emerge within a few blocks of the iconic *Apollo Theatre*.

• *MTA Today, New York City Transit Edition, 8/11/14*

Walking Distance: 125th Street Business Improvement District; The Studio Museum in Harlem; The National Jazz Museum in Harlem; Schomburg Center

Barclays Center

http://www.barclayscenter.com

Back in the late 1950's, before the Dodgers actually left Brooklyn for Los Angeles, the area around Atlantic and Flatbush Avenues, which sat right on a number of subway lines, as well as the Long Island Railroad, was considered to be a superb spot for the team to relocate, in hopes of staying in the Borough of Churches. Well, that never happened. The Dodgers went west and the proposed site stayed pretty much the same for half a century, except for a few stores being added. Then another professional team's move brought sports at the highest level back to Brooklyn, about a block from where the new Ebbets Field might have stood. The National Basketball Association Nets, originally a Long Island (and ABA) entity and lately a New Jersey resident, built a brand new arena and brought big time hoops to Brooklyn. Recently, I joined a number of Transit workers at the brand new Barclays Center.

The Barclays Center, which stands about 50 yards from the entrance to the B, D, N, Q, R, 2, 3, 4 and 5 subway lines, hits you right in the eyes, as soon as you walk through the front doors. Upon entering, you immediately hear the sound of music blaring and the sight of the huge scoreboard right in front of you. Essentially, you are about halfway between the arena floor and the upper seating area. To your right and left are corridors which lead you on a tour of diverse eateries in the Main Concourse area, with a Brooklyn flavor clearly in the mix. There are stands for Brooklyn Burgers, Nathan's hot dogs and Junior's desserts. There is also the Bed Stuy Grill, Paisano's Meat Market and the Avenue K Deli. After grabbing something to eat, you can head out into a fabulous arena, in which even the seats at the top of the building are not that bad. While the lower levels are similar to many older basketball/hockey venues, that is, cresting in a slight oval, the top decks are more tiered and thus not as far away as say, the upper reaches of Madison Square Garden. Overall, Barclays provided a wonderful night, with constant energy not only during the game, but between whistles, highlighted by the *Brooklynettes*, the Nets' dancing cheerleader troupe.

For a first time visitor, Barclays Center proved to be a great place to watch a game. You could even stand behind a rope just beyond the mid-level entranceway and watch the entire game from behind one basket. And though that night the home team succumbed in the end to the visiting Golden State Warriors, pro basketball in Brooklyn appears to have a bright future.

Along with the subway lines previously noted, the LIRR is also one block from Barclays Center.

- ***MTA Today, New York City Transit Edition, 1/11/13***

Walking Distance: Brooklyn Academy of Music (BAM); Junior's; Fulton Street Mall.

Beacon Theatre

http://www.beacontheatre.com

On West 74th Street, at 2124 Broadway, one of the last of the landmark theaters in New York City still stands, new and refurbished on the inside, but pretty much the same on the outside. The *Beacon Theatre*, which has been utilized for vaudeville, theatrical movies, concerts and various other entertainments, today continues a legacy of big-time show business, one which goes all the way back to 1929.

Designed by Chicago architect Walter Ahlschlager in the Art Deco style, the *Beacon Theatre* has long been renowned for its fabulous acoustics. Envisioned to be one of two "International Music Hall" theaters – the other being *Radio City Music Hall* – by theatrical impresario Samuel "Roxy" Rothafel, the *Beacon* did not reach the storied status of *Radio City*, but did maintain a level of excellence of its own. From its beginnings in vaudeville, opera and big screen movies, well into the days of musical concerts and comedy specials, the *Beacon* has vibrantly stood the test of time.

Among the highlights at the *Beacon Theatre* through the years are operatic performances of "Ballet on Broadway" in 1978 and "Madame Butterfly" in 1988, as well as a visit by the Dalai Lama in August of 1999. Artists like Michael Jackson, James Taylor, Aerosmith, George Carlin, Queen and Wanda Sykes have all played the *Beacon*. When the 1991 film "The Rolling Stones at the Max" played at the *Beacon*, it represented the first time that a concert hall had been fitted for IMAX. And on October 29, 2006, Bill Clinton was treated to a private Rolling Stones concert here, to help celebrate his 60th birthday. In recent times, the band most associated with the *Beacon Theatre* is the Allman Brothers Band, who played a block of concerts each March from 1989 to 2014, before finally closing out their career with a final show at the *Beacon* on October 28, 2014.

Unfortunately, anyone who went to a show at the *Beacon* in the past three decades could see that the old girl was deteriorating, though the acoustics remained strong. In November of 2006, MSG

Entertainment took over the *Beacon Theatre*. Since then, renovations have been made to this treasured hall, making it a much brighter venue for a more upscale 21st Century crowd. The *Beacon Theatre*, which was given landmark status by the *National Register of Historic Places* in 1979, remains a popular hall, one that New Yorkers and tourists alike should attempt to make a visit to.

The 1, 2 or 3 trains to the 72nd Street station – which has one of the great outdoor entrances in the City – leave you a few blocks from the *Beacon*. The M104 bus to 73rd and Broadway and the M79 to Broadway and 79th do the same.

- *MTA Today, New York City Transit Edition, 2/14/14*

<u>Walking Distance</u>: Central Park West; Lincoln Center for the Performing Arts; Stage 72 (at The Triad); New-York Historical Society; Avery Fisher Hall; American Folk Art Museum; American Museum of Natural History.

Brooklyn Academy of Music (BAM)

http://www.bam.org

Of all the artistic venues located in the city of New York, the *Brooklyn Academy of Music* is arguably the most refreshing and far reaching. Located in the heart of the Borough of Churches, both up and coming artists and craft masters can be found performing and/or exhibiting their art forms at *BAM,* whose three main buildings encompass various forms of expression.

The *Peter J. Sharp Building* at 30 Lafayette Avenue houses the *BAM Howard Gilman Opera House*, used for all forms of live performance, the *Lepercq Space,* the so-called "living room" of *BAM*, used for receptions, parties and meetings (and home to the *Bam Café*) and the *BAM Rose Cinemas*, a state-of-the-art facility used for film screenings, lectures and corporate meetings. All three active halls are available for rental use.

Bam Fisher is the home of the *BAM Fisher Hillman Studio*, a 1,600 square foot performance and event space, which provides working area for the *BAM* Cultural District, for both local and visiting artists. Also located at *BAM Fisher* are the *BAM Fisher Rooftop Terrace,* featuring the *Stutz Gardens* (where year round outdoor performances under a retractable enclosure may be held), and the *Fishman Space*, the newest performance area, which holds 250 people.

The *BAM Harvey Theater*, a few blocks from *Sharp* and *Fisher* at 651 Fulton Street is *BAM*'s all-purpose movie theater, where retrospectives of various actors, directors, producers and film genres regularly appear.

The *Brooklyn Academy of Music* first appeared in 1861, as the home of the Philharmonic Society of Brooklyn. From its home on Montague Street in Brooklyn Heights, the original *BAM* saw appearances by the likes of Mark Twain (1884) and Booker T. Washington (1891). When the Montague Street venue burned down in 1903, a new home in Fort Greene was eventually erected at the current 30 Lafayette

Avenue location. During the first year there in 1908, dancer Isadora Duncan provided one of the highlights. In over 100 years since (with two buildings added), *BAM* has remained a most celebrated home of progressive and avant-garde performances. Always a splendid place to view art of all kinds, *BAM's* facilities contain a vibrant backdrop for not only performance, but also creativity and development.

The 2, 3, 4, 5, B, D, N, Q and R trains to Atlantic Avenue/Barclays Center leave one just a short walk to the *Brooklyn Academy of Music*. The 4 and 5 to Nevins Street, the C to Lafayette Avenue and the G to Fulton Street also leave you within walking distance of *BAM*. The B25, B26, B41, B45, B52, B63 and B67 buses all stop within three blocks of *BAM*.

• *MTA Today, New York City Transit Edition, 8/29/14*

Walking Distance: Barclays Center; Junior's; Fulton Street Mall.

Brooklyn Cyclones at Coney Island

http://www.brooklyncyclones.com

Over a half-century ago, Brooklyn was defined by three icons: the Brooklyn Bridge, Coney Island and the Brooklyn Dodgers. In 1958, the Dodgers moved west and in 1964, Steeplechase Park, the last of the great Coney Island amusement parks, closed down for good. In the ensuing decades, the Great Bridge carried on, while old Dodger fans mourned their loss and Coney Island, though still on the map, deteriorated into a place that lost its luster and went almost silent when the sun went down. In 2001, as part of a territorial rights agreement between the Mets and Yankees, professional baseball returned to Brooklyn, albeit at the Single "A" level. What's more, the new *Brooklyn Cyclones* would be playing in a small (7,500 capacity) yard situated on the former site of Steeplechase Park, just a few blocks from Nathan's, the Atlantic Ocean and the classic rollercoaster that the team was named after. Playing in the short-season (76 games) New York-Penn League, along with their fellow newcomer and instant rival, the Staten Island Yankees, the Cyclones would soon become an institution themselves. As well as bringing back baseball to Brooklyn, one of the sport's greatest venues, the planting of the Cyclones on Coney Island also spurred a renaissance in the former waterfront haven.

With heightened security in the area, in response to the opening of the Cyclones' home field, Keyspan Park (since re-named MCU Park), the re-birth of Coney included new restaurants, a brand new Luna Park and the overall cleaning up of the area. The boardwalks, once glass-infested and dirty, are now immaculate, the new game/ride areas meld with the two classic leftovers, the Wonder Wheel and the Cyclone rollercoaster. (In 2014, a new Thunderbolt rollercoaster opened, just beyond the left field wall.) As for the ball club, after winning the NYPL Championship in their Inaugural season of 2001, the Cyclones have consistently packed them in, setting yearly attendance records, while making the play-offs just about every season. A Cyclones game is a step back in time, as the family crowd and the carnival atmosphere created by numerous between inning games and prizes give the visitor a taste of how baseball felt on all levels, before money changed the Major League landscape. The constant quality giveaways (jerseys, t-shits, bobbin' head dolls, etc.) are also a great reason to head down to a Cyclones game, with all ticket prices less than $20 a person.

Make it a point to take the D, F, N or Q trains this Summer to Stillwell Avenue, for a day at the beach, a ride on an iconic (or new) rollercoaster, a whirl on a classic Ferris wheel and a look at possible upcoming Major League stars at MCU Park. If you go on a Friday or a Saturday, the Coney Island fireworks show follows every game.

•   *MTA Today, New York City Transit Edition, 7/20/12*

Walking Distance: Gargiulo's Restaurant; Deno's Wonder Wheel Park; Luna Park; The Cyclone; Coney Island USA; New York Aquarium.

Central Park Zoo

http://www.centralparkzoo.com

One of the great venues of summer in *The City* is the fabulous *Central Park Zoo*. Though considerably smaller and certainly less heralded than its neighbor up in *The Bronx*, the *Central Park Zoo* is, nonetheless, a most wonderful habitat to spend a few hours, amongst a varied population of animals and landscapes. Through the years, it has evolved into an incredibly pleasurable place for both tourists and New Yorkers alike, if only to step away from *The City* itself.

I returned to the *Central Park Zoo* on a Saturday morning recently, about 7 years since my last visit, when I went with my Goddaughter Jackie, her husband Dave and their 3-year old daughter Nadiya. I found the evolution of the Zoo, which I had noticed in 2006, had continued. The map you received upon purchasing your ticket served to guide you through the few disparate areas on the grounds, though I chose to just wander up and down the pathways, without a concrete plan. Eventually, I had traversed all that this simple tribute to wildlife would allow.

On one side of the *Zoo* is the *"Tropic Zone,"* an enclosed area which featured birds and small animals that one might find in a warmer climate. On the other is the *"Polar Circle,"* which took you to the other extreme, showcasing polar bears, penguins and sea birds. In between, an area called the *"Temperate Territory"* featured ducks, snow monkeys, swans and fabulous little red pandas that seemed to meld the two surrounding habitats. In the center of it all is the wonderful sea lion pool, where you can see these active creatures constantly swimming and jumping in and out of the water. If you time it right, you can even catch a feeding, which is a singular treat.

Complementing the main *Zoo* is the *Tisch Children's Zoo*, featuring sheep and goats that the smallest children can feed, while getting their first taste of a zoo. To round it all out is the *4-D Theater*, which requires an extra fee that I'd wholly recommend. The movie currently showing is *"Dawn of the Dinosaurs,"* a delightful short animated film about a sloth who steals some dinosaur eggs and suffers the consequences. And what exactly is 4-D? Well, suffice it to say you're going to get wet, which is quite refreshing on a hot day.

To get to the *Central Park Zoo's* Main Entrance on 64th Street, the M1, M2, M3, M4, M5, M30 and Q32 buses stop on Fifth Avenue, between 59th and 64th Streets. The N and R trains to Fifth Avenue/59th Street and the 6 train to 68th Street/Hunter College all leave you just a few blocks from the *Zoo*.

- ***MTA Today, New York City Transit Edition, 8/23/13***

Walking Distance: The Woolman Rink; Shakespeare in the Park; FAO Schwarz; 107th Infantry Memorial; Asia Society & Museum; The Museum of American Illustration.

Cirque du Soleil – Totem
(at Citi Field through May 12)

http://www.cirquedusoleil.com/en/welcome.aspx

In 1984, a new type circus arrived from Canada. Founded by two former street performers, Guy Laliberte and Gilles Ste-Croix, _Cirque du Soleil_ ("Circus of the Sun" in English) combined a mix of circus acts with high octane street entertainment. Originally called _Les Echassiers_, which toured Quebec in 1980, _Le Grand Tour du Cirque du Soleil_ capitalized on a successful 1984 tour to fund a second season. Laliberte then hired Guy Caron from the _National Circus School_ to transform _Cirque_ into a character-driven show, devoid of the usual circus animals. This defines the _Cirque_ today as the contemporary circus ("nouveau cirque") that Caron envisioned.

Cirque du Soleil, which remained successful in the remainder of the 1980's, expanded drastically in the 1990's and 2000's, going from 1 to 19 shows, seen in over 271 cities in every continent except Antarctica. Each show combined circus styles from around the world with a central theme and storyline. Shows which featured the music of The Beatles (_"Love,"_ 2006), Elvis Presley (_"Viva Elvis,"_ 2009) and Michael Jackson (_"Michael Jackson: The Immortal World Tour,"_ 2011) now line the Las Vegas strip, taking _Cirque du Soleil_ to an even broader audience. A second Michael Jackson-themed show, _"Michael Jackson: One,"_ will begin previews on May 23rd. In and around the New York area, Cirque has begun to make its presence known as one of four popular circuses, along with _The Big Apple Circus_, the _UniverSoul Circus_ and the longest running of them all, the _Ringling Brothers & Barnum and Bailey Circus_.

After the success of _Cirque du Soleil: Zarkana_ which premiered at _Radio City Music Hall_ on June 29, 2011, a new show, _Cirque du Soleil: Totem_, began what was to be a three-week run at _Citi Field_ in Flushing in mid-March of this year. _Totem_ has since been extended until May 12th, which happens to be Mother's Day. On Friday, March 29th, I was fortunate enough to see _Totem_ with my niece Jaclyn and her son Alex. It was a night to remember.

Cirque du Soleil describes the theme of *Totem* (which premiered in Montreal in June of 2010) as *"the evolution of mankind from its primordial, amphibian state toward the aspiration of flight, taking inspiration from many of mankind's founding myths."* What I saw was an incredible display of acrobatics, backed by a fine light show and an inspired musical score. It would be pointless to try and describe all the acts, but I would highly recommend a trip to see any *Cirque du Soleil* troupe.

Cirque du Soleil – Totem and other subsequent shows have been located in a tent within the Citi Field parking lot. The 7 train to the *Mets-Willets Points* station drops you right there.

- ***MTA Today, New York City Transit Edition, 4/12/13***

<u>*Walking Distance:*</u> See: **A Trip to Citi Field** and **Radio City Music Hall & Rockefeller Center**, the two most frequently-used venues for *Cirque du Soleil*.

Exploring the Southern Tip of Manhattan

http://statueofliberty.org

Of the many fabulous sights, attractions and localities in New York City, the area around the Southern tip of Manhattan is one of the most vibrant and exciting, for a tourist or a lifetime resident. If you choose to wander to the deepest part of Downtown Manhattan, you can take a ride on a few ferry lines, tramp through one of New York's most underrated parks or happen by a number of free to very light on the wallet museums. The *Staten Island Ferry (SIF)*, which offers a refreshing 30-minute ride between Manhattan and Staten Island, is also a great way to take a unique look at the *Statue of Liberty* in New York Harbor. The *Statue Cruises* (just a short walk to the right of the *SIF*), take millions of visitors a year to the famous statue given to the United States by France (and dedicated in 1886), as well as to *Ellis Island*, where immigrants of all backgrounds were once screened and admitted into the country. At the *Ellis Island Immigration Museum*, the history of entrance into the United States via New York is celebrated. Amongst the many exhibits, there is an area where visitors can look up the records of a descendant who came into the country via this facility. Tickets for the *Statue Cruises* are sold at *Castle Clinton*, America's first immigration station (predating *Ellis Island*), where more than 8 million people arrived in the U.S. from 1855 to 1890. Beyond the islands Liberty and Ellis (or Governor's Island, the less heralded destination of a third area ferry), there are a number of other attractions within walking distance, after you've returned to the isle of Manhattan.

Battery Park, which includes the *Statue Cruises* ferry landing, also features the *East Coast Memorial*, which pays tribute to U.S. servicemen who died in coastal waters of the western Atlantic Ocean during World War II, and several other memorials. *The Sphere*, taken from the wreckage of the *World Trade Center*, still resides just inside the entrance to *Battery Park* and hopefully will remain there. Across from the park's entrance is the former *U.S. Customs House*, which now serves as a (free admission) branch of the *National Museum of the American Indian*. Within a short walk, in either direction, one can also find a number of other museums, including the *New York City Police Museum*, the *Museum of Jewish Heritage*, the *Skyscraper Museum* and the *Fraunces Tavern Museum*, which also doubles as a unique restaurant dedicated to the American Revolution.

The easiest way to get to Manhattan's Southern tip is by subway. The 1 Train (*South Ferry Station*), the 4 or the 5 (*Bowling Green Station*) and the R train (*Whitehall Street Station*) all leave you right in the heart of the area.

- **MTA Today, New York City Transit Edition, 9/18/12**

Walking Distance: New York Korean War Veterans Memorial; Pier 6 Helicopter Rides; 9/11 Memorial & Museum; New York Vietnam Veterans' Memorial Plaza; Trinity Church.

Getting to Carnegie Hall

http://www.carnegiehall.org

As any lifetime New Yorker knows, the notion of seeing everything that can be seen in the most vibrant city in the world is a daunting and yes, impossible task. As the years go by, one can hopefully manage to go and see as many of the unique and wonderful sights that *The City* has to offer. On January 12, 2013, I took another place off my personal checklist when I visited *Carnegie Hall* for the first time in my life, to see a group called *"1964:The Tribute,"* a band formed in 1984 that Rolling Stone hails as *"The Greatest Beatles Tribute Band on Earth."* While I can now vouch for the fact that Rolling Stone has a legitimate claim, I can also say that *Carnegie Hall* is unquestionably a great auditorium to see any kind of music (or other entertainment).

Carnegie Hall, located on 57th Street and 7th Avenue, opened in 1891, the result of a meeting four years earlier between industrialist Andrew Carnegie and the conductor of the Oratorio Society of New York, Walter Damrosch. Convinced by Damrosch to build a new musical venue for New Yorkers, Carnegie bought nine parcels of land on 56th and 57th Street, along 7th Avenue. On May 13, 1890, the cornerstone was put into place and roughly $1.1 million later (mostly out of Carnegie's pocket), *Carnegie Hall* opened with a five-day musical festival, which commenced on May 5, 1891. For more than a century since, *Carnegie Hall* has presented not only musicians, but great public orators and (later) comedians. Mark Twain, Vladimir Horowitz, Theodore Roosevelt, Maria Callas, Paul Robeson, Liza Minnelli, Bob Dylan and George Carlin have all appeared at the *Hall*, along with countless other symphony orchestras.

Carnegie Hall consists of three presentation halls: a 2,800 seat Main Hall, known today as *The Stern Auditorium/Ronald O. Perelman Stage*, a 600-seat Recital Hall below the Main Hall, called *The Judy and Arthur Zankel Hall* and a 250-seat Chamber Music Hall, *The Joan and Sanford Weill Recital Hall*, located adjacent to the Main Hall. The acoustics and intimate atmosphere of the Main Hall, where I saw *"1964: The Tribute,"* proved most remarkable. I'm quite sure the two smaller halls are even more personally riveting. There was also a small café connected to the left rear of the Main Hall, where many patrons ran for refreshments at intermission. A 16-piece strings and horns orchestra backed the Beatles tribute band for the second half of the show, which gave a taste of how well *Carnegie* could present diverse sounds. Overall, *Carnegie Hall* struck me as a grand auditorium. I'm glad I finally got there, *without practicing.*

The 57ᵗʰ Street stop on the N, Q and R trains leaves you right across the street from *Carnegie Hall.*

- *MTA Today, New York City Transit Edition, 2/1/13*

Walking Distance: Central Park South; Carnegie Deli; Stage Deli; Broadway Theater District; Museum of Arts & Design; Museum of Modern Art (MoMA); Paley Center for Media; Radio City Music Hall; Top of the Rock Observation Deck; Rockefeller Center.

Helicopter Rides from Pier 6

http://www.newyorkhelicopter.com

Ever since arriving at 2 Broadway in 2005, I have been of a mind to explore the entire area, mostly on foot. But there have been a few other modes of transportation that I vowed to look into at some point, like the double-decker buses that rifle down Broadway before heading back uptown, the water taxis and small boats that run tours in the waters around the lower tip of Manhattan and the helicopters that do the same from the skies up above. On my 52nd birthday, I finally went on a 15-minute flight around the bowels of *The City*, all the way up to 59th Street or so. From my vantage point, it was a trip well worth the wait.

New York Helicopter is one of three different copter tours that run out of *Pier 6*, which is located just to the Northeast of the Staten Island and Governors Island ferry slips. (The other two are called *Helicopter Flight Services* and *Liberty Helicopter*.) *New York Helicopter* features three separate tours, lasting approximately 15, 19 and 25 minutes. From this particular service, I chose the 15-minute flight around the lower tip of Manhattan and up the Hudson River. The time seemed to go quickly, as I took a barrage of photos, all along the route. The pilot, a guy named Aaron, kept a very steady pace, making it easy to center up all the great sights along the way for some once-in-a-lifetime pictures. I managed to get spectacular shots of the Statue of Liberty, the Empire State Building, the Brooklyn, Manhattan, Williamsburg and Verrazano-Narrows Bridges, as well as a wonderful panoramic view of the Southern tip of Manhattan, with the new Freedom Tower rising up at the former World Trade Center site. The term "whirlwind tour" comes to mind when I think of that flight now.

Though I truly enjoyed and would recommend the *New York Helicopter* service, I would urge anyone interested in taking a flight on a helicopter service which runs out of *Pier 6* to check them all out, as to rates and times, so as to fit what your particular preferences might be. From a helicopter over *The City*, things have an almost surreal feel to them. I'm sorry I waited so long to try a copter ride and I'm imagining I'll go up again one day, hopefully with a friend whom I've inspired to do the same.

The R or N trains to Whitehall Street, the 1 to South Ferry and the 4 or the 5 to Bowling Green all leave you within walking distance of *Pier 6*, where the Downtown Heliport is located.

- *MTA Today, New York City Transit Edition, 3/22/13*

Walking Distance: Staten Island Ferry; Governors Island Ferry; New York Vietnam Veterans' Memorial Plaza; South Street Seaport; Fraunces Tavern; National Museum of the American Indian/New York; Battery Park.

High Line

http://www.thehighline.org

While *Central Park* is one of the most famous parks in the world and the pride of New York City, another most unique park has sprung up in recent times in the Borough of Manhattan. The *High Line*, which is located on the footprint of an elevated freight line from another time, is a relatively new jewel in *The City's* green landscape. Running from Gansevoort Street in the meatpacking district to West 34th Street, between 10th and 12th Avenues, the *High Line* offers one a walk in the park which is straight, engaging and extremely scenic.

Built in the 1930's, the *High Line* was utilized to remove dangerous trains from the streets of Manhattan's largest industrial district. The declining use of railroads through the decades made the *High Line* less and less useful and the final trains ran there in 1980. After years of debate on whether to demolish the line, the *Friends of the High Line* was founded by Joshua David and Robert Hammond, residents of the *High Line* neighborhood, in 1999, to advocate for the *High Line's* preservation and reuse as a public open space. In 2009 and 2011, sections of the *High Line* re-opened to the public as park space. In September of 2014, the final section, *High Line at the Rail Yards*, opened, completing the run of this unprecedented city park.

There are a number of entrances where one can access the *High Line*. Stairways on West 18th, 20th, 26th and 28th Streets are complemented by entranceways containing elevator access on Gansevoort, 14th, West 16th, 23rd, and West 30th Streets. A temporary entrance on 34th street accompanied the opening of the final section in 2014. An eclectic string of *High Line* food vendors are located between West 15th and West 18th Streets and two *High Line* gift shops, on West 16th and 30th Streets, serve to enhance the experience of walking the *High Line*.

A walk on the *High Line* today is a most refreshing New York excursion, featuring a wide range of art, flowers and plant life. The new *Rail Yard* segment, with its winding turns, has added a significant layer of wonder to a truly unique park.

Subway lines that leave you within walking distance of one of the *High Line's* entrances include the A and the L (to 14th Street/8th Avenue), the C or the E (to either 14th or 23rd Streets at 8th Avenue) the 1 (to either 14th, 18th or 23rd Streets and 7th Avenue) and the 2 or the 3 (to 14th Street/7th Avenue). As for buses, the M11 to Washington Street or 9th Avenue, the M14 to 9th Avenue and the M23 or M34 to 10th Avenue also stop near *High Line* hubs.

- ***MTA Today, New York City Transit Edition, 12/12/14***

Walking Distance: Chelsea Market; Union Square; Theodore Roosevelt Birthplace; Madison Square Garden; Javits Center

Irish Hunger Memorial

http://www.bpcparks.org/bpcp/parks/parks.php#top

Of the many simple yet stark memorial areas in New York City, the *Irish Hunger Memorial*, located in Battery Park City at Vesey Street and North End Avenue, is one of the most thought inspiring, even if you are not Irish. Of course, my background did make this place quite a visceral assignment for me, especially upon going there after a few actual trips to the Emerald Isle.

The *Irish Hunger Memorial*, which takes its name from the Irish term for the famine that plagued the country from 1845-52, *"An Gorta Mor"* (*"The Great Hunger"*), was dedicated on July 16, 2002 on a half-acre site bordering the Hudson River. Designed by artist Brian Tolle, with the help of landscape architect Gail Wittner-Laird, it was commissioned as a contemplative site, serving to raise awareness of that tragic time and place, which led directly to a mass migration of the Irish to the United States. A parallel mission of the *Irish Hunger Memorial* was to serve as a catalyst for addressing world hunger in recent and current times.

As you walk down Vesey Street, to the right of the World Trade Center (now *9/11 Memorial*) site, the patch of seemingly out of place greenery (in the midst of the concrete City) suddenly shoots up in front of you, as you approach North End Avenue. To enter the *Memorial*, you have to walk around the raised parcel of land, to a tunnel at the rear which contains various relevant quotes from the time of the Irish Famine, as well as more recent quotes and facts about world hunger today. When you emerge into the light, you first encounter a large County Mayo cottage, which was brought across the pond and reconstructed, along with stones, soil and native vegetation from the southern part of Ireland. Stones from all 32 counties of Ireland are represented on the authentic landscape that Tolle and Wittner-Laird designed.

The *Memorial* winds up a pathway to a peak which allows one to look down at a landscape true to how it appears in Ireland today, or to turn around and overlook the majestic Hudson River. A simple, understated and somewhat curious venue, the *Irish Hunger Memorial*, which began construction in March of 2001, in the very shadows of what was not yet called Ground Zero, would nonetheless be completed and dedicated by July of 2002, even as the World Trade Center site was being cleaned up.

To get to the *Irish Hunger Memorial,* take the A, C, J, Z, 2, 3, 4 or 5 trains to Fulton Street or the N or R to Cortlandt Street, walk north to Vesey Street, make a left and proceed a few blocks to North End Avenue. The E to World Trade Center, a block south to Vesey Street and the same few blocks do the same.

- *MTA Today, New York City Transit Edition, 1/17/14*

<u>Walking Distance</u>: 9/11 Memorial & Museum; The Anne Frank Center/USA; City Hall Park; Trinity Church; Canyon of Heroes.

Junior's

http://www.juniorscheesecake.com

Though I have no intention of being a food critic in these pages, there are a few eateries which are New York City icons. And though places like the *Carnegie Deli* in Manhattan or *Terrace on the Park* in Queens are historic in their own right, the one restaurant in New York City that I would urge anyone to make a point of visiting is *Junior's*, home of the best cheesecake in New York, as well as fine lunch and dinner menus. Over the years, *Junior's* has added Manhattan sites in Grand Central Station and the Times Square area, but it is the original home, at the corner of Flatbush Avenue Extension and DeKalb Avenue in Downtown Brooklyn, which is the one and only *Junior's* that must be experienced.

Founded by Harry Rosen in 1950, at the site of where a diner had been run by his family since 1929, *Junior's* quickly grew from a local to a national restaurant of note, mostly due to their *"Most Fabulous Cheesecake and Desserts."* In the 1950's, *Junior's* cheesecake became as big a Brooklyn classic as a hot dog at *Nathan's Famous* in Coney Island. From early on, many visitors, famous or obscure, included a slice of *Junior's* Cheesecake on their New York "to-do" list. The celebrated dessert has been mentioned in pop culture many times over the years.

Today, *Junior's* remains a most fabulous place to either sit down and eat or pick up some great take-out meals and desserts. The bowl of pickles at each table and the photos of Brooklyn on the walls are signature items at *Junior's*. Burgers, sandwiches and the London broil are all recommended. Different varieties of cheesecake, fruit pies and other desserts are all served in healthy portions. The take-out window and in-house bakery, both located right inside the corner entrance, each offer fresh items to go, in a timely fashion. The bar near the side entrance is a good place to wind down or wait for a table when the restaurant is packed.

On the day before Thanksgiving each year, you will always find a line of people outside *Junior's*, wrapped around the block onto the Flatbush Extension, as holiday revelers make their annual pilgrimage for post-turkey desserts. (I always go on Tuesday to beat the rush.) But whatever your sensibilities, I would highly recommend a trip to *Junior's* at some point, especially if you are making the rounds of classic New York venues. In February of 2014, Junior's prepared to sell this landmark site to realtors in the condo market, though they were negotiating a deal to return to this original site at a later date, while a new Brooklyn site (as yet undetermined) was being utilized. Eventually, the Rosen family decided not to sell. Amen.

The main entrance to the DeKalb Avenue station on the D, N, Q and R lines leaves right across the street from *Junior's*. The 2, 3, 4 and 5 trains to Nevins Street leave you a few blocks away.

- *MTA Today, New York City Transit Edition, 2/21/14*

<u>Walking Distance</u>: Fulton Street Mall; Metrotech Business Improvement District; Brooklyn Academy of Music (BAM); Barclays Center.

Macy's/Herald Square

http://www.visitmacysnewyork.com

There are many great museums in New York City. There are numerous Broadway theaters, restaurants and a few great ballparks. And though there are some other Macy's stores, there is only one *Macy's/Herald Square*. *The City* is certainly not at a loss for places to shop and large department stores, though less prevalent than they once were, can still be found. Nonetheless, on 34th Street in Manhattan, the "miracle" spoken of in a movie title over 65 years ago continues to be a reality.

Built in 1902, *Macy's/Herald Square* was the first building in the world to have modern day escalators. Those classic wooden escalators, with the large "teeth," are still in use today in parts of the store. The traditional *Macy's Thanksgiving Day Parade* made its first appearance in 1924, the same year that the completed 7th Avenue wing of the store made the Herald Square location *"The World's Largest Store,"* a title still used today, though the Shinsegue store in Centun City, Busan, South Korea surpassed it in surface area in 2009.

"R. H. Macy Dry Goods" first opened in 1851 in Haverhill, Massachusetts, to serve local mill industry employees. The chain, originally four stores, took off when it moved to Sixth Avenue and 14th Street in New York City in 1858. In 1895, Isidor and Nathan Straus, who previously sold china and other goods out of what was now "R. H. Macy & Co." bought Macy's and moved it to the 34th Street and Herald Square location, where it eventually expanded to cover the entire square block of 34th and 35th Streets and Herald Square and Seventh Avenue, with the exception of a pair of small existing businesses on the perimeter.

The 1947 film *"Miracle on 34th Street"* made *Macy's/Herald Square* world famous and the scenes of the Thanksgiving Day Parade in that movie brought that attraction to a National audience. To this day, millions of New Yorkers make a point of going to this flagship store during Christmastime, to see the fabulous window displays, to bring their kids to see Santa Claus and quite frankly, to take themselves back to another Era. A walk through *Macy's/Herald Square*, particularly during the holidays, gives the visitor a unique feeling of timelessness. At any time of year, though, *Macy's/Herald Square* is a New York wonder, one that must be seen to be felt, be you a relentless shopper or just a wandering soul.

The 34th Street/Herald Square train station services the B, D, F, N, Q and R lines. The 1, 2, 3, A and E trains to 34th Street/Penn Station leave you a block away.

• *MTA Today, New York City Transit Edition, 12/13/13*

Walking Distance: Madison Square Garden; Penn Station; Empire State Building; Times Square; Bryant Park; New York Public Library; Grand Central Terminal.

Madison Square Garden, Through the Years

www.thegarden.com

Currently the oldest venue being used for National Hockey League games and the second oldest for National Basketball Association games (next to the Oracle Arena in Oakland), *Madison Square Garden* has had a long and gloried history of sports and entertainment in both its current home and the three previous sites where *The Garden* has been housed. A widespread assortment of musical talent has performed there and as the 21st Century turned, the moniker *"The World's Most Famous Arena"* seemed to be a pretty good fit, even as recent renovations have made *The Garden* a somewhat different place than in its heyday.

The original *Madison Square Garden* was located in Madison Square, where two different venues called *Madison Square Garden* flourished, one from 1879-1890, the other from 1890-1925. Six-day bicycle races were a big event during this period. *The Garden* then moved to Eighth Avenue, between 49th and 50th Streets, where it remained from 1925-1968. This third MSG was the site where the legend of *The Garden* grew, with the Ringling Brothers and Barnum & Bailey Circus serving as an early main attraction. The NHL Rangers and the NBA Knickerbockers were also regulars, but boxing probably became the most famous event seen regularly at the Hell's Kitchen address.

In 1968, the fourth and current *Madison Square Garden* opened, between 31st and 33rd Streets and 7th and 8th Avenues, above the modified, underground Pennsylvania Station, which had been demolished on the main level, where *MSG* would now stand. The Westminster Kennel Club Dog Show, a *Garden* staple that had begun in the early days, emerged as a huge event in this fourth *Garden*. Three signature nights at the current *MSG* will always stand out as special. The Knicks won their first NBA Championship on May 8, 1970, (before adding a second title in 1973). The Rangers, who went to the Stanley Cup Finals in 1972 and 1979, won their first Stanley Cup since 1940 on June 14, 1994 at *The Garden*. And on March 8,

1971, Joe Frazier defeated Muhammad Ali in one of the most famous heavyweight title matches in boxing history.

In recent times, the New York Liberty of the WNBA have called *MSG* home, and three separate renovations have added two overhanging balconies, which beckoned to the days of the tiered *Garden* in Hell's Kitchen. Recently, New York's own Billy Joel has become *The Garden's* first "house musician," signing on to play a concert once a month.

The A, C, E, 1, 2 and 3 trains to 34th Street/Penn Station leave you underneath *The Garden*, while the B, D, F, M, N, Q, and R trains to 34th Street/Herald Square are just an avenue away.

- ***MTA Today, New York City Transit Edition, 9/19/14***

Walking Distance: Penn Station; Macy's Herald Square; Empire State Building; The High Line; Times Square.

MLB All-Star Fan Fest at Javits Center

http://www.javitscenter.com

In 2013, the *Major League Baseball All-Star Game* celebrates the 80th Anniversary of the Inaugural match, held in 1933 in Chicago's Comiskey Park. For the ninth time, a New York team will be the host city, which in recent times means not just the game itself, but also a number of related events. Before the game takes place on the night of Tuesday, July 16th at Citi Field, the home of the Mets, there are two other *All-Star* attractions at the ballpark. On *All-Star Sunday*, July 14th, there is a *Futures Game*, which pits some of the top Minor League prospects from various organizations, in a USA vs. The World format. There is also an *Old Timers/Celebrity Softball Game* on Sunday. On Monday night July 15th, the very popular *Home Run Derby* comes to Citi Field, with eight sluggers – four from the NL and four from the AL – vying for the yearly long ball title. Of all the *ASG* events though, the most accessible is the *MLB Fan Fest*, which will be held in the *Jacob Javits Center*, from Friday, July 12th, through Tuesday, July 16th.

This year, a *New York National League* team will host the *All-Star Game* for a fifth time, with the Mets doing the honors for a second go around. In 1934 and 1942, the New York Giants hosted the *ASG* at the Polo Grounds and in 1949, the Brooklyn Dodgers held the game at Ebbets Field. In 1964, the Mets' original Queens' home, Shea Stadium, hosted the game in its Inaugural season. On the American League side, the Yankees hosted the game in 1939 and 1960 in the original (1923-1973) Yankee Stadium and in 1977 and 2008 in the refurbished (1976-2008) Stadium. The *MLB Fan Fest* and all the other contemporary additions to the All-Star "experience' were first seen in New York for the 2008 *ASG*, in Yankee Stadium II's final season.

As the events at the ballpark are much harder to get into (unless one is a ticket plan holder or of a mind to pay big bucks to an online scalper site), the *MLB Fan Fest*, which runs only $35 for adults, is the one affordable way to be a part of what will be an exciting extended weekend for baseball fans and curious onlookers. The *Javits Center*, located on 11ᵗʰ Avenue, between 34ᵗʰ and 40ᵗʰ Streets, is an established convention hall, one that can properly display all the baseball-themed activity that will adorn it in July.

The A, C and E trains to 34ᵗʰ Street/Penn Station and the 1, 2, 3, 7, B, D, F, N, Q and R trains to 42ⁿᵈ Street/Times Square all leave you a few blocks walk from the *Jacob Javits Center*.

- ***MTA Today, New York City Transit Edition, 6/21/13***

Walking Distance: Madison Square Garden; Penn Station; Empire State Building; Intrepid Sea, Air & Space Museum; Circle Line Sightseeing at Pier 83; Times Square.

New Yankee Stadium/Macombs Dam Park

http://newyork.yankees.mlb.com/nyy/ballpark/index.jsp

In September of 2008, when the Yankees played their final game at the grounds which housed the Original Yankee Stadium (1923-1973) and the refurbished model (1976-2008), the *new Yankee Stadium*, located right across the street, was in the final stages of construction, preparing for an April 2009 opening. While many ballparks have made similar "next door" moves to brand new yards in the past decade or two, the unique aspect of moving this institution of *The Bronx* was that the new *Stadium* would be built on the grounds of the former *Macombs Dam Park*, which opened in 1899, or 24 years before the *Original Yankee Stadium* opened in 1923. In April of 2012, a brand new *Macombs Dam Park* finally opened, with two beautiful new fields and one side practice field. Though this project took a while to get done, when they finally completed the park, it was a wonderful place for young people to play ball, once again in the shadow of *Yankee Stadium*.

As for *Yankee Stadium III*, the new park is much like many built in the last 20 years on the Major League circuit, in that it provides visitors the ability to walk all around the lower deck and watch the game, a staple of the modern "open air" ballparks. While they made this yard much in the image of the previous two incantations, it does have updated amenities, such as a few large restaurants incorporated into the grounds (the most notable being the *Hard Rock Café*, located near the main entrance by the "4" elevated line and the *Mohegan Sun Restaurant*, which unfortunately hampers the view of the updated version of the revered *Monument Park* in centerfield). There is also more than one message/information board, including a giant screen in right center which is absolutely the best one in baseball. As for history, the Yankees celebrate their vaunted existence with a *Great Hall*, where a parade of huge banners honor all the pinstripe greats, from Ruth and Gehrig to DiMaggio and Dickey, to Mantle, Ford and beyond. There is also a *Yankees Museum*, which houses artifacts from each great *Era* of the franchise, plus statues of pitcher Don Larsen and catcher Yogi Berra, symbolically situated 60'6" apart, which collectively celebrate what is to date the only *Perfect Game* in World Series history. Display cases filled with autographed balls fill in the area between the Larsen and Berra statues and seats from all versions of *Yankee Stadium*, plus the locker of beloved catcher Thurman Munson round out a most special shrine.

The opening of *Macombs Dam Park* makes the area of 161st in The Bronx complete again. A ride on the "4" El or the subway "D" is still the best way to get to *The Stadium* or The Park.

- ***MTA Today, New York City Transit Edition, 6/29/12***

Walking Distance: Grand Concourse; Bronx Museum of the Arts; Louis Heintz Memorial in Joyce Kilmer Park.

New York City Center

http://www.nycitycenter.org/Home

Among the many cultural centers in New York City, one of the most endearing is *New York City Center*, located on 55th Street, between 6th and 7th Avenues. For over 70 years, *City Center* has been at the forefront of artistic venues in Manhattan, ever since then Mayor Fiorello LaGuardia introduced it in 1943.

The current home of *City Center* was originally called the *Mecca Temple*, when it was built in 1923 by architect Harry Knowles, along with the firm of Clinton & Russell. The *Mecca Temple* housed Shriners' meetings, which had previously been held in *Carnegie Hall*. After the Wall Street crash of 1929, the Shriners could not keep up the tax payments on the *Temple* and the site became city property. By the 1940's, scheduled for demolition, the Neo-Moorish building was rescued by LaGuardia and New York City Council president Newbold Morris, who revived it as a center for performing arts, Manhattan's first such institution.

Over the years, many theatrical presentations have been held at *City Center*. Stars that have performed there include Gwen Verdon, Helen Hayes, Charlton Heston, Celeste Holm, Hume Cronyn and Jessica Tandy. Also, various dance troupes have called *City Center* home, such as the New York City Opera (1944-66), the New York City Ballet (1948-66) and the Joffrey Ballet (1966-1982).

Today, *City Center* is the home of the Alvin Ailey American Dance Theater. Since 1984, the Manhattan Theater Club has been on site, with two small (150- and 299-seat capacity), recently renovated stages located adjacent to the main hall. In 1994, *City Center* held the first of its *Encores! Great American Musicals in Concert* productions. This extremely popular program carries on to this day and in 2013, spawned *Encores! Off-Center*, featuring Off-Broadway musicals through the eyes of contemporary artists. In addition, a 2011 renovation of the main stage revitalized and modernized this historic theater.

The *New York City Center Education Department* provides accessible arts education to various schools and communities in NYC. Each year, over 8,000 public and private school students take part in dance and musical theater performances and in-school performance workshops through *City Center*. Through the *Introduction to Performing Arts* program, students have the opportunity to view live performances at *City Center* and mini-residences and full residences offered there provide different levels of learning about live performance art.

The N, Q and R trains to 57th Street/7th Avenue, the F train to 57th Street/6th Avenue and the D and E trains to 7th Avenue/53rd Street all leave you a few blocks from *New York City Center*. The M1, M2, M3, M4, M5, M6, M7, M10, M20, M31, M57 and M107 buses all have stops near *City Center*.

- *MTA Today, New York City Transit Edition, 9/16/14*

Walking Distance: Carnegie Hall; Central Park South; Carnegie Deli; Stage Deli; Broadway Theater District; Museum of Arts & Design; Museum of Modern Art; Radio City Music Hall; Top of the Rock Observation Deck; Rockefeller Center.

New York Hall of Science

http://www.nysci.org

If the conscious goal of our public buildings and exhibitions is to educate, inspire and entertain our children, then the *New York Hall of Science* in Flushing, Queens is one of the best museums we have in *The City*. Located in *Flushing Meadows- Corona Park*, the *NYSCI*, as it is known, has grown gradually over the years from when it first opened as a pavilion for the *New York World's Fair* of 1964-65.

At the time of its opening, the *NYSCI* was one of only a few science museums in existence. When the *World's Fair* ended, unlike most other pavilions of the *Fair*, the *NYSCI* remained as a learning facility for students until 1979, when it was closed for renovations. Re-opening in 1986, the center became more about science in everyday life, then in the science fiction world originally conceived in the 1960's. Further renovations and expansions began in 1991 and 1996, when a new entrance, a Science Playground and a dining area were commissioned. In 1999, the rockets originally donated to *Rocket Park* in *NYSCI* by the U.S space program were restored; a mini golf course was eventually added within *Rocket Park*.

On returning to the *NYSCI* for the first time in decades, I was struck by the amount of young people flowing throughout the building. It was a Thursday morning and they had just opened, but there were already three busloads of school children in the museum, with a total of six more arriving by the time I left, an hour and a half later. The *NYSCI* was filled with simple experiments and displays that kids could look at and experience, first hand. So many properties of science could be explored, from the effects of light and shadow to various interactive probabilities to the space program, which was so predominant when they first opened in 1964. There was even a singular display case which celebrated that long ago *World's Fair*, which the existence of the *NYSCI* honors on a daily basis. If you have children, I would highly recommend this most unique and fabulous museum. For me, it was like going home again, to a place I had been to as a young boy and later, as a teenager. The old wavy-shaped building still stood, yet had been expanded substantially, making for a totally different museum than I had known, yet one that was even more inspiring.

NYSCI is a short walk from the 111th Street stop on the 7 train or the Q48 bus which stops right under the 7 on 111th Street and Roosevelt Avenue. The Q23 or Q58 buses to Corona Avenue and 108th Street also leave you just a few blocks away.

- *MTA Today, New York City Transit Edition, 3/18/13*

Walking Distance: Queens Museum; Terrace on the Park; Queens Zoo; USTA Billie Jean King National Tennis Center; Citi Field.

Paley Center for Media

http://www.paleycenter.org

Originally called the *Museum of Broadcasting* and later *The Museum of Television & Radio*, the *Paley Center for Media*, located at 25 West 52nd street, between Fifth and Sixth Avenues, provides a wealth of vintage broadcast programming, which can be readily accessed. Founded in 1975 by William S. Paley, the man who built the Columbia Broadcasting System (CBS) into the most successful radio and television network, the original *Museum of Broadcasting* building was at 1 East 53rd Street, right on 5th Avenue. When they changed their name to *The Museum of Television & Radio* in 1991, they moved to their current home, which was then called the *William S. Paley Building*. In 2007, the building was renamed *The Paley Center for Media*. There is also a branch of the *Paley Center* in Beverly Hills, California, which opened in 1996.

Television and radio shows are added to the *Paley Center's* collection as they are discovered or donated by individuals or organizations. There are frequent seminars and interviews with industry notables at the *Center*. All of them are taped and put into the archives, for visitors to view at a future date. On the main floor, there is a bookstore/gift shop and the *Steven Spielberg Gallery*, which is used for exhibitions, receptions and fund-raising events. But the lifeblood of the venue comes in the form of dozens of computers on the fourth floor library, where visitors can access up to an hour and a half of programming, before either giving way to others who have been waiting or being themselves given a second viewing period, if the number of computers available exceeds the current number of visitors.

When I went recently, I watched parts of three shows. The first was a *Westinghouse Studio One* production of the original version of the jury drama, *12 Angry Men*. I also watched a clip of comedian George Carlin on *The Tonight Show with Johnny Carson* from the early 1970s' and part of an ABC documentary which showed the actions of President John F. Kennedy and Attorney General Robert

F. Kennedy versus Alabama Governor George Wallace, who was preparing to block the path of two young black students attempting to integrate the University of Alabama in June of 1963. I found all three shows by making a quick search on the desktop.

The B, D, F or M trains to 47th-50th Street, the E train to Fifth Avenue and 53rd Street and the N or R trains to 49th Street all leave you just a few blocks from the *Paley Center for Media*. Buses running Southbound on Fifth Avenue, Broadway and Seventh Avenue and Northbound on Madison Avenue and Avenue of the Americas (6th Avenue) all have stops near or at 52nd Street.

- ***MTA Today, New York City Transit Edition, 6/28/13***

__Walking Distance__: Museum of Modern Art (MoMA); Broadway Theater District; Times Square; Top of the Rock Observation Deck; Radio City Music Hall; Saks Fifth Avenue.

Radio City Music Hall & Rockefeller Center

http://www.radiocity.com   http://www.rockefellercenter.com

Originally slated to be called the "International Music Hall" before its opening in December of 1932, *Radio City Music Hall* has been, for eight decades and counting, one of the premiere New York showplaces. Through the years, the familiar building on the corner of 50th Street and the Avenue of the Americas (6th Avenue) has seen stage shows, movies, concerts and the world famous *Christmas Spectacular*, featuring the high kicking Rockettes, a *Radio City* fixture since its inception. Though it was briefly in peril of being closed down and turned into office space in the 1970's, *Radio City Music Hall* survived and became greater than ever. In the past few decades, it has hosted award shows (Grammys, Emmys), talk shows (David Letterman), game shows (Jeopardy) and live sports (New York Liberty WNBA basketball). Currently operated by Madison Square Garden, inc., live music concerts and the *Christmas Spectacular* are still the predominant entertainments at *Radio City Music Hall*, the most recognized of the buildings in the *Rockefeller Center* complex.

Spanning 48th Street to 51st Street, between 5th and 6th Avenues, *Rockefeller Center's* original (1930's) complex of 14 commercial buildings are known for their art-deco style architecture. An additional four buildings were added in the 1960's and 70's, although to this day, the area is defined by the GE (formerly the RCA) Building, which houses the NBC Studios, where live shows, like *Late Night with David Letterman*, *Saturday Night Live* and *The Today Show* have originated. The local NBC NEWS broadcasts live from *Rockefeller Center* and there are often live morning concerts in the streets outside *The Today Show* set.

Every Christmas season, *Rockefeller Center* renews its proper place as a most famous New York holiday venue. A giant Christmas tree is trucked in, planted in the square above the iconic *Rockefeller Center* ice rink, decorated and then lit up on national television. The tree lighting show, in fact, which began as a modest half-hour special, has morphed into a 2-hour extravaganza, featuring singers, the Rockettes and both real and imagined celebrities. The *Top of the Rock* observation deck, some 70 stories high, offers a fine view of Manhattan, second only to the Empire State Building, from the top of the GE Building. The famous "Lunchtime atop a Skyscraper" photo (with workers sitting across a girder, 840 feet above ground) was taken at the then RCA Building in 1932 and that image is now used on a wide assortment of gifts (candy bars, mouse pads, etc.) sold in the *Top of the Rock* gift shop.

The B, D, F and M trains go to the 47th-50th Street/Rockefeller Center stop and the N, Q and R trains on the 49th Street stop also leave you just a block away.

- *MTA Today, New York City Transit Edition, 12/14/12*

Walking Distance: Museum of Modern Art (MoMA); Broadway Theater District; Times Square; Paley Center for Media; Saks Fifth Avenue.

Remembering Shea Stadium
and the World's Fair

http://www.worldsfaircommunity.org

In April of 1964, the two-year old New York Mets moved into their brand new ballpark, *Shea Stadium*, a yard built to resemble the *Colosseum* in Rome. This event coincided with the opening of the *New York World's Fair*, right across the way in *Flushing Meadows-Corona Park*. For the next two years, the *World's Fair*, the last ever held in New York City, entertained millions, while the Mets, though an extremely poor team, did the same. Having filled the void left by the loss of the New York Giants and the Brooklyn Dodgers, who abandoned *The City* in 1958, the Mets fueled the growing need for National League baseball in New York. The *Fair*, set up right in the midst of the burgeoning U.S. Space program, featured many futuristic attractions. The one-two punch of the Mets and the *World's Fair* made the #7 Flushing Elevated Line more prominent than it had ever been, since the late 1920's when it first stretched to the *Main Street, Flushing* station, just one stop after what (in 1964) would become the *Willets Point/Shea Stadium* station. In addition, when the Beatles played at *Shea* on August 15, 1965, it launched the age of outdoor ballpark concerts. So anyone around and conscious in the years 1964-65 can still maintain a vivid memory of the *Fair* and early days of the Mets. Then a few things changed.

The *World's Fair* closed after the 1965 season and the Mets struggled for a few more years, until a new manager hired in 1968, former Brooklyn Dodger great Gil Hodges, led them to an unexpected World Championship in 1969. The Mets would go on to win three more National League Pennants (1973, 1986 and 2000) at *Shea*, including a second World Title in 1986. U.S. Open Tennis would arrive in *Flushing Meadows* in 1978, on part of the former *World's Fair* site. *Shea Stadium* was razed in the winter of 2008-9, after 45 seasons as the home of the Mets.

Today, you can still find remnants of the Summer of 1964. In the parking lot to the left of the main entrance to the Mets new home, *Citi*

Thomas Porky McDonald

Field, you can find markers notating the former site of *Shea* pitcher's mound and four bases. In *Flushing Meadows*, the iconic *Unisphere* and the *New York Hall of Science* (featuring *Rocket Park*) remain from the *1964-65 World's Fair.* A ride on the #7 Elevated Line is still the best way to go and see these landmarks, right alongside current attractions, like *Citi Field*, the *Billie Jean King National Tennis Center* and the *Queens Museum*, which has actually been around since the *1939-40 World's Fair.*

- *MTA Today, New York City Transit Edition, 7/6/12*

___Walking Distance___: Flushing Meadows-Corona Park, USTA Billie Jean King National Tennis Center; Queens Museum, Queens Zoo, New York Hall of Science, Main Street shopping district.

Schomburg Center for Research in Black Culture

http://www.nypl.org/locations/schomburg

Located on 135th Street in Harlem, the *Schomburg Center for Research in Black Culture* is one of the leading research facilities dedicated to studying African-American, African Diaspora and African experiences. A well respected branch of the New York Public Library, the *Schomburg Center* serves as both a classroom and a storehouse for the diverse nature of people of color, past, present and (ideally) future.

The collections of Arturo Alfonso Schomburg, which date back over 85 years ago, formed the origins of the *Schomburg*, which has grown to be a significant hub for the cultural life of Harlem itself. In 1926, when Schomburg's personal collection was incorporated into the New York Public Library's 135th Street branch, few could have imagined what a far-reaching effect this venue would become in the decades to come. There are a number of areas in the *Schomburg Center* available for research purposes.

The *Research and Reference Division* contains more than 150,000 volumes and 85,000 microforms, which are mostly in English, though they also include works in a variety of African and European languages. The *Manuscripts, Archives and Rare Books Division* contains more than 3,900 rare books, 580 manuscript collections, and 15,000 pieces of sheet music and rare printed materials. The *Art and Artifacts Division* includes paintings, sculptures, works on paper and textiles, and material culture. It contains more than 20,000 items from Africa and the African people. The *Photographs and Prints Division* includes more than 500,000 items, including portraits of many prominent 19th- and 20th-century black artists, political figures, actors, musicians, athletes, and social activists. The *Moving Image and Recorded Sound Division* offers a broad range of audio-visual documentation of black culture including music, oral history recordings, motion pictures, and videotapes. It offers over 5,000 hours of oral history recordings and more than 5,000 motion pictures and videotapes of early black documentaries and radio programs from many parts of the world. All of these resources can be accessed by contacting the *Schomburg Center* and stating your particular study and/or research needs.

There are always three or four thought-provoking exhibits on display at the *Schomburg*, with an expansive collection of diverse art, film and poetry often in the mix. Workshops and free public events are constantly on the calendar, so it is best to check their website as to what is current and upcoming on the schedule. The *Schomburg Shop* offers up a revolving bevy of merchandise and is notable for its gift ideas during the Holidays and for *Black History Month*.

The 2 and 3 trains and the M7 and M102 buses to 135th Street all leave you right outside the *Schomburg Center for Research in Black Culture.*

- *MTA Today, New York City Transit Edition, 11/21/14*

Walking Distance: Apollo Theater; Studio Museum in Harlem; St. Nicholas Park.

Stage 72 (at The Triad)

http://stage72.com

Formerly known as *The Triad*, a recently refurbished entertainment venue offers New Yorkers the chance to see some interesting acts, as well as iconic City performers, for a very reasonable price. They call it *Stage 72*.

Located on 72nd Street just off Broadway, *Stage 72 at the Triad* is a very small hall (capacity: 130) situated on the second floor of a building that features a Mediterranean restaurant on the main floor. With small tables and mini-booths, it has the feel of the old comedy clubs that used to thrive in the 1970's and 80's. (This is understandable since one of *Stage 72's* proprietors is Rick Newman, the former owner of *Catch a Rising Star*, a place that most people I know went to at least once, back when huge and up and coming acts regularly filled that comedy club.)

When it was known as *The Triad*, musicians (Gregg Allman, Joan Osbourne), comedians (Tracy Morgan) and long running Off-Broadway shows (*Forbidden Broadway*) all appeared on their stage. Newman and *The Triad's* Peter Martin completed a five-year renovation of the club in November of 2012. Since then, the new *Stage 72 at the Triad* has been offering up all kinds of solid entertainment, including a recurring show called *Celebrity Autobiography*, in which City actors and comedians read verbatim from actual celebrity autobiographies, which leads to absolute hilarity.

I was made aware of *Stage 72* when I recently saw an advertisement in one of the free papers which now envelop the City. (Those free papers, for my money, are much more useful in finding things to do in New York than any of the established newspapers.) This particular ad cited a one night appearance by long time stand-up comic Richard Belzer, who would be doing a new act called "*Richard Belzer's Rock & Roll Comedy Extravaganza*." Belzer, who has been starring on television as Detective John Munch for the past two decades, first on *Homicide: Life on the Street* and currently on *Law & Order: Special*

Victims Unit, was right back at home doing stand-up. In this act, he gave comic impressions of Mick Jagger, Keith Richards, Bob Dylan, Bruce Springsteen and others. In between, he told some great stories and was generally as funny as I remembered him to always be. The intimate setting at *Stage 72* made for a fabulous evening. You can find out about and buy tickets for all the upcoming shows on their website. I would highly recommend a visit to *Stage 72.*

The 1, 2, 3, B or C trains to their respective 72nd Street stops all leave you a short walk from *Stage 72 at the Triad.*

• ***MTA Today, New York City Transit Edition, 5/17/13***

<u>Walking Distance</u>: Beacon Theater; Central Park; Lincoln Center for the Performing Arts; New-York Historical Society; Avery Fisher Hall; American Folk Art Museum; American Museum of Natural History.

The Empire State Building Experience

http://www.esbnyc.com

The *Empire State Building* is still – for many New Yorkers – the greatest building in the world and the perfect symbol for *The City* itself. For forty years, it was the tallest building in the world and though many other structures surpassed it in the 1970's and beyond, the *Empire State Building,* constructed during the *Great Depression,* remains a most remarkable edifice.

From the time that the Eiffel Tower in Paris arrived in 1889, at 984 feet high, there was a race to the sky, as "building vertical" became a reality, especially in the United States. The culmination of that Era began on March 17, 1930, when construction started on what would become the *Empire State Building,* on the site of the original Waldorf-Astoria hotel. Using some innovative ideas, like a railway built at the site to transport materials quickly and a hopper that ultimately fed 10 million bricks to floors as needed, the construction of the *Empire State Building* was a wonder of efficiency. Considering that all of the buildings which surpassed the *ESB* took *years* to construct (the first being the World Trade Center in 1973), the 14 months it took to finish the jewel on 5th is amazing (*ESB* opened on May 1, 1931). That this all occurred during the *Depression* is even more astonishing, although of course this project created thousands of jobs, in a time when people were not going to miss even a day of work, in fear of someone else taking their place.

Two early objectives of the building were not reached. Office space for businesses did not thrive until the 1950's and the plan to use the antenna spire as a mooring dock for the popular dirigibles of the day proved fleeting. Tourism, however, characterized the *ESB* and was a hit from the very first. In 1964, floodlights were added to illuminate the top of the building, and to this day, the green lights on St. Patrick's Day or the red, white and blue ones on Independence Day are just two of the many color themes that are utilized each year.

Standing 102 stories and 1,250 feet high (1,454 feet counting the antenna spire), the *Empire State Building* may not be the tallest building in the world anymore, but it is arguably the most recognizable. The phenomenon of my ears popping on the elevator up and the stunning views from the 86th Floor Observatory Deck (first encountered when I was a young boy) remain among the great thrills of *The City* for me (and millions of others).

The 34th street – Herald Square station on the B, D, F, M, N, Q and R trains leaves you just a block away from the *Empire State Building.*

- ***MTA Today, New York City Transit Edition, 12/21/12***

<u>*Walking Distance:*</u> Macy's Herald Square; Madison Square Garden; Penn Station; Times Square; Bryant Park; New York Public Library; Grand Central Terminal.

The Forbes Galleries

http://www.forbesgalleries.com

If you are in the 14th Street/Union Square area, you might want to veer off the path a few blocks to 12th Street and 5th Avenue, for a most engaging free mini-museum, located on the first floor of the Forbes Magazine Building. *The Forbes Galleries*, a group of interwoven rooms filled with rotating exhibits from the collection of the magazine's longtime publisher, Malcom Forbes, can provide a refreshing momentary stop off the concrete kingdom outside. In the 1970's, Forbes, who was known as a collector of many things, began displaying some of the art he had acquired in the ground floor of the offices of the magazine founded by his father, B. C. Forbes, in 1917. After Malcolm Forbes' death in 1990, *The Forbes Galleries* carried on, and does to this day.

When I arrived there on a Saturday morning recently, I was struck by the organization of it all. The main entrance to the magazine's offices are separate from *The Forbes Galleries*, with welcome banners leading you into the halls containing the current items on display from Forbes' prized collection. An exhibit called *Out of This World! Jewelry in the Space Age* contained an impressive array of space-related trinkets and baubles of all price ranges. There were earrings, pins and necklaces which reflected the sun, the moon or the stars, including a group of "Halley's Comet" broaches. Watches made for astronauts to take into space, along with other jewelry that was simply brought along on different missions by the space travelers, spiced up the exhibit, but the centerpiece for me was one of three miniature models of Apollo 11's Lunar Excursion Model (LEM), created by Cartier Paris and given to each of the members of that historic journey. The LEM on display originally belonged to Michael Collins, the Command Module pilot.

The other notable exhibit was called *Monte-Carlo Legends* and contained a vast collection of photos featuring some big name celebrities like John Wayne, Kirk Douglas and Steve McQueen in and around the hot spots of Monaco. The shot of McQueen at the 1965

Monaco Grand Prix, along with renowned driver Jackie Stewart, reminded me of the star's love of racing. Suffice it to say that *The Forbes Galleries* presented a most interesting fork in the road, one I'd recommend wholeheartedly.

The 14th Street stations of the 1, 4, 5, 6, A, B, C, D, E, N and R trains all leave you just a few blocks from *The Forbes Galleries* on 12th Street and 5th Avenue. From Uptown, the M1, M2 and M3 buses to 14th Street and 5th Avenue do the same, as does the Downtown M6 bus to 14th Street and Sixth Avenue.

• *MTA Today, New York City Transit Edition, 1/10/14*

Walking Distance: Union Square Park; Washington Square Park; Strand Bookstore; Theodore Roosevelt Birthplace; The Rubin Museum of Art; The National Arts Club; The Center for Jewish History.

The Ride

http://www.experiencetheride.com

In New York City, the attractions are numerous and widespread. Some of them are more famous than others, some are bigger, some smaller, some seemingly personalized and some pointedly more universal. Many of them have been around for a very long time, for years, decades, even centuries. But every once in a while, something comes along that presents New York in a new and decidedly different way. One of the most recent of these is a bus tour run out of Times Square called *The Ride*.

An hour and a half whirlwind tour taken in the largest vehicle allowed in the streets, a 45-long, 14-foot wide and 8-foot tall bus, *The Ride* is part theater and part performance art, with a good dose of comedy, planned and unrehearsed, in the mix. Wandering deliberately through a 4.2 mile stretch of *The City*, people in the street become part of the show, whether they were meant to be or not. A pair of on-board hosts/guides, known as Jackie and Scott, lead the mobile audience through various landmarks of New York, while an array of street performers step out of the crowd to enhance this most unique trip through Gotham.

The Ride took its first tours in October of 2010, after four years of development by a group of entertainers and entrepreneurs, led by a man named Michael Counts. By 2011, new CEO Richard Humphrey fashioned a corporate staff which stretched the marketing potential of the venture and by May of 2012, they were even offering a special Summer edition called *The Fazzino Ride*, which showed New York City through the eyes of 3D pop artist Charles Fazzino, the official artist of the National Football League and the 2012 Olympics. The positive public reaction to *The Fazzino Ride* is evident, in that other thematic *Rides* are being prepared for future dates.

A most creative hybrid performance piece, *The Ride* is unlike anything else in the tourism landscape of New York City. State of the art audio and video within the bus, including a very representative subway stop simulation, makes *The Ride* a wonderful attraction for tourists, while the native New Yorkers can also revel in the feel of *The City* that *The Ride* encapsulates.

You can get tickets online or at *The Ride* box office, which is located in Times Square, on 42nd Street, between 7th and 8th Avenues, right next to *Madame Tussaud's Wax Museum*. *The Ride* originates from the corner of 42nd and 8th Avenue, in front of *Chevy's Mexican Restaurant*. The 1, 2, 3, A, C, E, N, Q and R trains to 42nd Street all stop at or within a block of *The Ride* launch point.

- *MTA Today, New York City Transit Edition, 7/25/14*

Walking Distance: Port Authority Bus Terminal; USS Intrepid Sea, Air & Space Museum; Bryant Park; New York Public Library; Grand Central Terminal; Macy's Herald Square; Madison Square Garden; Penn Station.

Theodore Roosevelt Birthplace

http://www.nps.gov/thrb/index.htm

There are some places in the City of New York that many of us who have lived here all of our lives miss out on, simply due to a lack of research. If we knew that certain venues existed, we would surely (or hopefully) take the time to drop by and if for but a moment, enhance our lives. Such a place is the *Theodore Roosevelt Birthplace*, the site where TR became the only President of the United States born in New York City. The three-story re-created brownstone, located on 28 East 20th Street in the Flatiron District houses not just memories, but a visceral feeling which cannot be properly described without actually going there.

The modest townhouse in the middle of the block sticks out amongst the much taller buildings that surround it. The original home was demolished in 1916, but following Roosevelt's death in 1919, the *Women's Roosevelt Memorial Association* rebuilt it and refurnished it with most of the original pieces, which were preserved before the demolition and then supplied by TR's sisters and wife for the re-creation.

Young Theodore, known as *"Teedie,"* was a sickly child who suffered a bad case of asthma, forcing him to be a home schooled lad who longed for the great outdoors. He found his adventure in the many books he read while in this house, which he lived in until age 14. His father, who taught him that wealthy people such as themselves should give something back to the community, was instrumental in the formation of the *American Museum of Natural History*. At the *Theodore Roosevelt Birthplace*, you can stand in the spot where that most famous New York museum was founded in 1869, as well as the bed where Teddy Roosevelt was born.

There is a 25-minute video about the life of Theodore Roosevelt which is shown in the basement level, where the entrance is. Every hour there is a tour of the period rooms on the first and second floors, where you can take non-flash photos. It is a fascinating look back to a time and place where someone who really left his mark on this country and the world was reared. The adult Roosevelt, the very physical head of the *"Roughriders,"* can be even more appreciated when you see the obstacles he had to overcome as a child, albeit a rich one.

The R and 6 trains to 23rd Street and the N, Q 4 or 5 trains to Union Square/East 14th Street all leave you a short walk to the *Theodore Roosevelt Birthplace National Historic Site*. The M1, M2, M3, M5 and M23 buses to their various 23rd Street stops do the same.

- *MTA Today, New York City Transit Edition, 5/31/13*

Walking Distance: Union Square Park; Madison Square Park; The Forbes Galleries; Strand Bookstore; The National Arts Club; The Center for Jewish History; The Rubin Museum of Art.

Times Square in the 21st Century

http://www.timessquarenyc.org/index.aspx

They still drop the ball at 11:59 PM each December 31st to ring in a New Year and the streaming message ticker still passes on local and world news. The crowds have remained daunting, frenetic and enthusiastic. But *Times Square*, one of the great New York icons, has taken on a radical change in the past few decades, to the point of being almost unrecognizable to those who nervously purveyed those streets in the 1960's, 70's and 80's. Back then, *Times Square* – at night – was heralded as much for its seediness as it was for being the lighted front porch to the New York theatre scene. And while some would debate whether the area is better or worse in the 21st Century, all would agree that it is certainly *different*.

Times Square these days includes a whirlwind tour of places to dine. On 42nd Street, a huge *McDonald's*, with hand painted murals, a diorama of the New York City skyline and a replica of the Statue of Liberty, is the most basic of all the local eateries. Barbecue lovers can feast at the multi-level *Dallas BBQ* restaurant. (If you're lucky enough to get a second floor seat close to a window, the view of *Times Square* is fabulous.) As you walk from the *Deuce* on down to 50th street, you can find countless other places to have a bite, ranging from *Bubba Gump's Shrimp* to the *Hard Rock Café* to one of the remaining dirty water hot dog vendors that still can be found on selected street corners. You may not run into too many people who know what an *Orange Julius* is, but you can get a *Jamba Juice*, if you're of a mind.

As for entertainment, *Times Square* is still at the heart of the Broadway district and discounted tickets to all the current (and upcoming) shows in the area can be purchased at the big *TKTS* booths in the center of the *Square*. Other fine attractions include a pair of gems located right next door to one another on 42nd, *Madame Tussaud's Wax Museum* and *Ripley's Believe it or Not Odditorium*. Directly across from these unique museums is *B.B.King's Blues Club and Grill*, which consistently offers the finest live music in the area. A pair of regular weekend attractions, the *Beatles Brunch* on

Saturdays (featuring a top *Beatles'* tribute band, *Strawberry Fields*) and the *Sunday Gospel Brunch* (with the *Harlem Gospel Choir*), offer two of the best deals in Manhattan ($40 for all-you-can-eat brunch and equally uplifting shows). Places to shop are everywhere, be you a tourist or not.

Though some might miss the adult entertainment world that *Times Square* once was, the current version caters to a much larger audience. The 1, 2, 3, A, C, E, N, Q and R trains all stop at or within a block of *Times Square*.

- ***MTA Today, New York City Transit Edition, 10/4/12***

__*Walking Distance*__: Port Authority Bus Terminal; USS Intrepid Sea, Air & Space Museum; Bryant Park; New York Public Library; Grand Central Terminal; Macy's Herald Square; Madison Square Garden; Penn Station.

USS Intrepid & Space Shuttle Pavilion

http://www.intrepidmuseum.org

When the space shuttle *Enterprise* was relocated to Pier 86, it further enhanced the recently refurbished *Intrepid Sea, Air & Space Museum Complex*, and a truly must-see attraction was realized. The *Intrepid* had been a great tourist and local hot spot since it first opened in 1982, but the addition of the new *Space Shuttle Pavilion* provided a new beginning to the *Intrepid* experience. The addition of the space shuttle accentuates the fact that the *Intrepid*, commissioned in 1943 and having served in WWII, had later been used as the recovery ship for two early NASA missions (*Mercury/Aurora 7* and *Gemini 3*). This linkage of where *Intrepid* began and evolved into made the trip to the big carrier in 2013 a particularly inspiring visit.

These days, the *Intrepid Sea, Air & Space Museum Complex* affords one many options. Besides the basic admission, you can also (for small fees) explore the strategic missile submarine *Growler* (featured with the *Intrepid* since 1989), the *British Airways Concorde* or the aforementioned *Space Shuttle Pavilion*. There are also audio tours, three simulators and four unique guided tours available. This innovative way of presenting the exhibits gives the visitor total command of exactly what they wish to see.

The *Intrepid* itself contains four decks which make up the story of the ship. The lower *Gallery* and *Third* decks offer up a look at life as a crew member of a U.S. carrier. The *Hangar Deck* is pretty much the main area of concentration, as history, technology and changing times are shown via ship hardware, storyboards and genuine and replica artifacts. The *Flight Deck* is probably the most emotionally effective, as you survey various fighter planes and copters that would have once been landing and taking off from the vast area that you are walking across. The *Flight Deck* is also where the *Space Shuttle Pavilion* is housed, taking up about ¼ of the deck's surface. The space shuttle *Enterprise* stands tall within this makeshift hangar, which also tells the story of the shuttle program through the years, not only the triumphs, but also the tragedies of *Challenger* and *Columbia*. In any case, a day at the *Intrepid Sea, Air & Space Museum Complex* is an exhilarating event.

The 42nd Street stops of the A, C, E, N, R, S, 1, 2, 3, and 7 trains all leave you within walking distance of the *Intrepid Sea, Air & Space Museum Complex* at Pier 86 on 46th Street & 12th Avenue. The crosstown M42 bus to 12th Avenue leaves you a few blocks closer and the M50 bus drops you right in front of the *Intrepid*.

- ***MTA Today, New York City Transit Edition, 3/7/14***

__Walking Distance__: Port Authority Bus Terminal; Times Square; Bryant Park; New York Public Library; Grand Central Terminal.

(2)

Museums

*Some of the many museums
found in The City*

American Folk Art Museum

http://www.folkartmuseum.org

If traditional folk art and the works of contemporary self-taught artists from the United States and abroad intrigue you, the *American Folk Art Museum* might well be the place for you. With items ranging from the 18th Century to the present, the *American Folk Art Museum* is an institution dedicated to the appreciation of traditional folk art. Portraits, sculptures, landscapes, seascapes, pottery, furniture, needlework and rugs highlight the museum's collection. A relatively modest museum, exhibitions change every few months, with a specific artist generally spotlighted. When I visited, the works of former slave Bill Traylor were at the centerpiece of it all.

There were two displays that celebrated the self-taught Bill Traylor (1854-1949), a man born into slavery on a plantation in Dallas County, Alabama, where he continued to live and work after Emancipation, until 1928. *Traylor in Motion: Wonders from New York Collections* gave an in-depth look at a particular group of Traylor's creations, which when viewed amongst one another, gave the viewer a feeling of motion, a movie-like sensation, as the pieces in question were all based on people and animals mulling about in Traylor's small town. *Bill Traylor: Drawings from the Collections of the High Museum of Art and the Montgomery Museum of Fine Art* contained over 60 drawings and paintings produced late in the artist's life. The contributions of Charles Shannon, a local young artist who made friends with Traylor (who was drawing on the streets when Shannon first encountered him), giving him art supplies and ultimately promoting the elderly man's work, rounded out the entire Traylor display. I had seen Traylor's work in passing in the past, without having known his name or his story, so these exhibits really hit home with me.

In an adjacent gallery, *Recent Gifts* contained just what it claimed to: 17 various pieces of art recently donated to the *America Folk Art Museum*. The treatment of the Traylor exhibits and the *Recent Gifts* collection spoke well of how future exhibitions, like *alt-quilts:*

Sabrina Gschwandtner, Luke Haynes, Stephen Sollins (opening in October) or *Folk Couture: Fashion and Folk Art* (which opens in January) might also positively move even a transient public. Overall, the *American Folk Art Museum*, including its gift shop near the entrance, was another nice stop on the road in *The City*, one that is free and would not take too long to check out, if you were to find yourself in the Columbus Circle area.

The 1 train to 66th Street/Lincoln Center leaves you right outside the *American Folk Art Museum.* In addition, the M5, M7, M11, M20, M66 and M104 buses all stop right near the Columbus Avenue and 66th Street venue.

- **MTA Today, New York City Transit Edition, 9/20/13**

Walking Distance: Lincoln Center; Avery Fisher Hall; Central Park West; Columbus Circle; Museum of Arts & Design; New-York Historical Society Museum & Library; American Museum of Natural History (AMNH).

American Museum of Natural History (AMNH)

http://www.amnh.org

Though it is a thrill to experience one of the many seemingly "hidden" museums or other places of interest in *The City*, returning to one of the "big dogs" is always a welcome attraction. And as far as museums go, there is none quite like the spectacular *American Museum of Natural History*. The majestic main entrance of the *AMNH*, located on Central Park West and 79th Street, featuring rooftop sculptures of Daniel Boone, James J. Audubon, Meriwether Lewis and William Clark looking down on a statue of former New York Governor and 26th President of the United States Theodore Roosevelt on horseback, fuels the inner excitement felt by children and adults alike, as they prepare to enter these most treasured halls.

Founded in 1869 by a number of benefactors, including Theodore Roosevelt Sr., the future President's father, the *AMNH* was originally housed in Central Park's Arsenal Building. The cornerstone for the current site was set in 1874 and in 1877, they opened the first of what would become 27 interconnected buildings, with 45 exhibitions halls, a planetarium and a library. The *AMNH* quickly became one of the signature museums in *The City* and remains so to this day.

Upon returning to the *American Museum of Natural History* recently with my friends and Transit co-workers Monah Johnson and Frank Rosa (along with Frank's almost 10-year old daughter, Gigi), I was once again enthralled by the incalculable wealth of exhibits that confronted us as we wound in and out of the corridors on all four floors of the establishment. Beyond the temporary exhibits, like *"Dark Universe"* at the Hayden Planetarium and *"Whales: Giants of the Deep,"* various halls chronicled and celebrated mammals, birds, reptiles, amphibians, Indians and other peoples of the world. Through all this, the one thing that still dominated the *AMNH* was the collection of dinosaur skeletons on the fourth floor, one of the great sights to see in New York City. The *Theodore Roosevelt Memorial* on the first floor, which was refurbished and re-opened in 2012, was another rare treat.

Three are four restaurants in the museum, with the Food Court in the Lower Level the most attractive. As it happens, a good friend and grammar & high school classmate of mine, Stephen Neligan, was the museum's Executive Chef at the time of my visit. Let's just say that I highly recommend the spread that Steve and his colleagues present daily.

The B (weekdays only) and C trains to the *81ˢᵗ Street/Museum of Natural History* stop lead you right to the Lower Level of the *AMNH.* The 1 train stops at Broadway and 79ᵗʰ Street. The M7, M10, M11, M79, M86 and M104 buses all leave you near a museum entrance.

- **MTA Today, New York City Transit Edition, 5/9/14**

Walking Distance: Central Park West; American Folk Art Museum; New-York Historical Society Museum & Library; Seventy Ninth Street Boat Basin; Children's Museum of Manhattan; Jacob's Pickles.

Asia Society & Museum

http://asiasociety.org

At the corner of Park Avenue and 70th Street rests a particularly vibrant cultural center, if a random visit in early Autumn can be trusted. The *Asia Society & Museum* not only housed some impressive artifacts, it also gave the feel of the far-reaching venue that it aspires to be.

Founded in 1956, the *Asia Society*, a non-profit, nonpartisan educational institution, has offices all over the world, including ones in Hong Kong, Manila, Los Angeles, Melbourne, Seoul, Houston, Mumbai, San Francisco, Shanghai, Washington D.C. and New York. Through the arts, culture, education and policy, the *Asia Society* strives to generate ideas, provide insights and promote collaboration in addressing present challenges among the peoples of Asia and the United States, which may secure a fruitful, shared future. Obviously, the New York venue is a vital one, if all of these goals are to be realized.

In the museum proper, an exhibit called *Iran Modern*, which will run until January of 2014, displayed artists of Iranian descent and their disparate art forms. Beginning with works from decades before the 1979 Revolution into current times, the exhibit takes up two floors of the *Asia Society* building, with artists associated with the Saqqakhaneh movement, the first culturally specific modernist group, whose works were influenced by both Shi'ite folk art and pre-Islamic art, featured prominently. Sculptor Parviz Tanavoli's use of copper and bronze particularly impressed me, as did the mirror mosaics of Monir Shahrody Farmanfarmaian, an artist who melds her Iranian heritage with modern Western geometric abstraction.

Though *Iran Modern* took up most of the floor space, a smaller exhibit, *Chinese Ceramics for the Islamic World*, was equally enticing, with shallow platters from the Yuan Period (1279-1368) at the forefront. An eye-catching 15th Century blue and white porcelain vase with a three-clawed dragon design represented the type of gifts once given to Persia. The *Chinese Ceramics* for the Islamic World display will also run into early January 2014. Overall, the rare and distinct pieces I saw at this wonderful Park Avenue site gave me a new enlightenment for art around the world, in places I would not normally be headed toward. In addition, there are also regular performances, lectures and symposiums at the *Asia Society & Museum*.

By bus, the M1, M2, M3 and M4 to Madison Avenue and East 70th Street, the M101, M102 to Lexington Avenue and East 70th Street, the M30 to Park Avenue and 72nd and the M66 to Park Avenue and 68th Street all leave you at or near the *Asia Society & Museum*. By train, the number 6 train to East 68th Street/Hunter College leaves you a few blocks away.

- ***MTA Today, New York City Transit Edition, 11/22/13***

<u>Walking Distance</u>: Whitney Museum of American Art; Central Park Zoo; Frick Art Reference Library.

Brooklyn Museum of Art

http://www.brooklynmuseum.org/home.php

There are museums of all sizes in New York City, with some known throughout the world. This pure volume and selective prominence does create, however, a situation where there are certain venues which really do not receive their just due. The *Brooklyn Museum of Art*, located in close proximity to a few other Brooklyn landmarks, is one of these. The fabulous *Brooklyn Botanic Gardens* and the festive Prospect Park and its zoo seem to be more recognized than this most impressive museum sitting in the midst of these almost iconic Brooklyn thoroughfares. But do not be mistaken, the *Brooklyn Museum of Art*, or simply, the *Brooklyn Museum*, takes a back seat to none, when you consider all that lies within its walls.

Full disclosure, I made my first ever trip to the *Brooklyn Museum* in the early Fall of 2013. Shame on me, because what I encountered that day reminded me why all New Yorkers should get out as much as possible and explore as many of the sites that the greatest city in the world has to offer. Beyond the usual spate of time-limited exhibitions, the permanent collections on display in the *Brooklyn Museum's* five floors treat the visitor to some of the finest art the world has known.

The *Great Hall* on the first floor features a fascinating area called *Connecting Cultures* and a sampling of the museum's *Art of Africa* collection. There is a café and sculpture garden located on the first floor as well. On the second floor, the scene shifts to another permanent collection, *Arts of Asia and the Islamic World*. The third floor, symbolically in the center of it all, is arguably the most impressive in the building. A four-walled collection of European paintings leads one toward one of the largest collections of Egyptian art in the world, including an *Ancient Egyptian Art* section and a spooky area known as *"The Mummy Chamber."*

The highlight on the fourth floor is the *Elizabeth A. Sackler Center for Feminist Art* and also houses period room re-creations, including representations of the 18th Century South, New England

and Brooklyn. On the fifth floor, the *Luce Center for American Art* offers artifacts as diverse as a statue of legendary engineer Robert Fulton to a pair of vases with images of John Adams and Thomas Jefferson painted on them. To be sure, there is plenty to see at the *Brooklyn Museum.*

The 2 or the 3 train to the *Eastern Parkway/Brooklyn Museum* stop leaves you right in front of the *Brooklyn Museum of Art.* By bus, the B41 or B69 to Grand Army Plaza and the B45 to St. Johns Place and Washington Avenue leave you a short walk away.

* *MTA Today, New York City Transit Edition, 5/24/14*

Walking Distance: Brooklyn Botanic Gardens; Prospect Park, Zoo & Carousel; Brooklyn Library; Grand Army Plaza; Soldiers and Sailors Memorial Arch.

El Museo Del Barrio

http://elmuseo.org

There are a number of museums and places of interest for people of various backgrounds in New York City. Each of them holds a part of the complete tale of *The City* in its domain. Maybe the most evocative of these is *El Museo Del Barrio,* or simply *El Museo (The Museum).* Artist and educator Rafael Montanez Ortiz founded *El Museo* over 40 years ago, with the assistance of a group of dedicated parents, educators, artists and activists. The group's realization that mainstream museums pretty much ignored the artistic contributions of the Latino Community spurred the creation of a museum dedicated to the Puerto Rican diaspora in New York City. Originally located in a P.S. 125 schoolroom at 425 West 123rd Street, *El Museo del Barrio* was later housed in a number of other venues, including a few storefronts on 3rd avenue between 107th and 108th Streets. In 1977, *El Museo* moved to its current location at 1230 5th Avenue between 104th and 105th streets, in the Heckscher Building. When I dropped by there recently, there was scaffolding up around the front of the building, which seemed to mirror the continuous evolution of *El Museo* itself.

By chance, my visit was on the third Saturday of the month, which in *El Museo* terms means it was "*Super Sabado,*" a day where admission is free and families are welcomed to a free arts and crafts workshop in the classrooms on the third floor. The museum itself also had plenty to offer interested parties who happened by.

El Museo La Bienel 2013 showcased the seventh edition of a growing tradition. Entitled "*Here is Where We Jump*" this year, *El Museo's* biennial exhibition featured various artists from *The City* and abroad. The title refers to a quote from one of Aesop's Fables, called "*The Braggart,*" in which a boast about a jump results in a challenge to repeat that jump. The paintings of Manuel Vega of the Bronx, and the sculptures of Bogota's Miguel Cardenas certainly considered a "jump" of sorts for the artists profiled. For me though, the most interesting piece I saw was a wall of composite police photos framed by San Juan's Ignacio Gonzalez-Lang called "*Guess Who?*"

which spoke to the possibilities of profiling. Overall, the works of the 38 artists represented in *La Bienel 2013* presented a tangible thought-provoking atmosphere.

The M1, M3, M4 or M106 buses to 104th Street or the M2 bus to 101st Street all leave you right near *El Museo Del Barrio*. The 6 train to 103rd Street or the 2 or 3 trains to Central Park North/110th Street also leave you just a few blocks away.

- *MTA Today, New York City Transit Edition, 12/27/13*

Walking Distance: Museum of the City of New York (MCNY); Central Park Conservatory Gardens; Harlem Meer.

International Center of Photography (ICP)

http://www.icp.org

All my life I have been a *City* wanderer, especially in Manhattan. I've walked from the East and Harlem Rivers across to the Hudson, covering a fairly large portion of that most unique landscape. So when I come across a new museum, one I've never seen, seemingly hidden in plain sight, I'm always quite amazed, yet pleasantly so. Such a place is the *International Center of Photography (ICP)*, a modest venue located in the heart of Midtown, on the corner of 43rd Street and the Avenue of the Americas (6th Avenue). I dropped by this two-floor display case for numerous photographers and producers of disparate images one Saturday recently and I was reminded of the creativity that the open lens allows.

Every three years, the *International Center of Photography* showcases an array of contemporary photography and video works. Toward that end, the *ICP* currently houses a rather impressive exhibit called *A Different Kind of Order: The ICP Trienniel*, which features 29 artists from around the world, with the world's current social, economic and political issues the central focus. A couple of these particularly caught my eye.

Two pieces from the *"Diorama Maps"* of Japanese photographer Sohei Nishino were very interesting, in that they portrayed their target sites, New York (from 2006) and Jerusalem (from this year) in large photo montages, bringing Manhattan and the heart of the Holy Land vibrantly alive. And my favorite offering in *The ICP Trienniel* was called *"Collective Lightboxes: 2008-2010,"* a photo spread inspired by a 54-story residential building in Ponte City, Johannesburg. This exhibit consisted of three vertical photo montages, each representing the building, with pictures of doors, windows and television sets, respectively, positioned in relatively the same place they resided in the building forming each "tower." A collaborative effort by South African photographer Mikhael Sobotzky and British artist Patrick Waterhouse, the *"Lightboxes"* were positioned along the stairs between the museum's two floors, which, by design or purely random placing, held the other exhibits together. *"A Different Kind of Order"* runs through September 22nd; I'd recommend giving it a look before it closes.

The ICP also has an affiliated school located diagonally across 6th Avenue from the museum, which serves over 5,000 students a year, with a range of courses, from digital media to darkroom practice. Seminars, symposiums and Youth programs are also available at the *ICP*.

The B, D, F, M and 7 trains to 42nd Street/Bryant Park and the 1, 2, 3, N, Q and R trains to Times Square all leave you a within a block or two of the *ICP*. The M5, M6 and M7 buses to 42nd Street and the Avenue of the Americas do the same.

- ***MTA Today, New York City Transit Edition, 8/5/13***

Walking Distance: Bryant Park; New York Public Library; Grand Central Terminal; Times Square; The Morgan Library & Museum; Empire State Building; Rockefeller Center; Top of the Rock Observation Deck; Radio City Music Hall; Museum of Modern Art (MoMA).

Jewels of Downtown Brooklyn

http://www.brooklynhistory.org museum   http://www.mta.info/mta/

After working in *Downtown Brooklyn* for 20 years, my department, like a number of others, moved to 2 Broadway in Lower Manhattan in 2005. When the aftermath of *Hurricane Sandy* recently left thousands of us without a worksite for a few weeks, many of us were fortunately afforded the opportunity to call 130 Livingston Street home once again. Simply put, Brooklyn still is a most magical place, at least for me. *Downtown Brooklyn* always inspired me, with two small but significant museums located a short distance from one another front and center. One day during our exile from Manhattan, I took a walk and recalled how much that area meant to me, especially those two jewels of *Downtown Brooklyn.*

The *New York Transit Museum*, located just across the street from the 130 Livingston Street offices, is one of the true hidden treasures of *The City*. Situated in an old train station, the *Transit Museum* offers a wonderful history of the subway system and the fleet of buses which have roamed *The City* for over a century. New exhibits open from time to time, while other aspects of the transit system remain permanently on display. Patrons buy their tickets at an old token both clerk station and a wonderful gift shop is located right near the entrance/exit. The museum holds numerous workshops for children and a small theater, whose entrance is the mock front of a "G" train, offers up educational presentations. Unquestionably though, the centerpiece of the museum is on the track level, where trains from all Eras line the tracks. Over the years, I have shown this museum to a number of friends and family and they have all been noticeably impressed. As a Transit worker, I feel the *Transit Museum* is something to take great pride in. (There is also a 20% discount on all sales for Transit workers.)

If the *Transit Museum* isn't the most underrated museum in New York City, the *Brooklyn Historical Society Museum* just might be. Standing on the corner of Pierrepont and Clinton Streets, the *BHS* shares the rich history of the fabulous Borough of Churches. Over the years, the Brooklyn Navy Yard, Coney Island, the Brooklyn Dodgers, the Brooklyn Bridge and Brooklynites themselves (including the fictitious *"Honeymooners,"* the Kramdems and Nortons of 328 Chauncey Street) have all been celebrated at the *BHS*. Currently, the centerpiece exhibit, *"Inventing Brooklyn,"* chronicles how the fabric of Brooklyn has been shaped through the years.

The Borough Hall Station, where the 2, 3, 4, 5, N and R trains run, leaves you a short walk (in either direction) to the *Transit Museum* or the *Brooklyn Historical Society Museum.*

- *MTA Today, New York City Transit Edition, 1/14/13*

<u>**Walking Distance**</u>: Jackie Robinson Plaque at Montague & Court; Brooklyn War Memorial; Brooklyn Promenade; Metrotceh Business Improvement District; Fulton Street Mall.

Merchant's House Museum

http://www.merchantshouse.org

One of the first 20 buildings designated as a *National Historic Landmark* when the landmark laws came into effect in 1965, the *Merchant's House Museum*, located at 29 East 4th Street, is considered one of the finest examples of architecture from the period of its birth in 1832. A museum for over 75 years, the *Merchant's House Museum* serves to educate as to how a wealthy merchant family (and their four Irish servants) lived there from 1835-1933. The Tredwell family is represented by furniture, decorative arts, clothing, books, housewares and personal effects. Over 3,000 items make up the Museum's collection, including 12 mahogany side chairs made by renowned cabinet maker Duncan Phyfe and over 40 dresses worn by the Tredwell women.

Upon entering the 19th Century home, you are given a binder which contains a guide to the four floors in the ancient edifice. The ground floor contains the recently renovated kitchen and the family room, highlighted by a large brick oven, as well as a cast iron stove that was installed later in the 19th Century. Highlights on the other floors include a pair of parlors separated by two old fashioned sliding mahogany doors that once kept the incoming visitors (front) apart from the those already in the house (rear), until the new guests were announced and greeted. A piano and the aforementioned Phyfe chairs decorate the parlors; candle stands, oil lamps and a pair of gas chandeliers represent the evolving manner of lighting used in the 1800's.

Impressively steep wooden staircases lead you up to the two grand bedrooms with floral canopy beds that dominate the upper floors. A writing desk that was used regularly by the Tredwells, in a time when letter writing was a main form of communication, is also prominent. The just recently re-opened servant's quarters, where the live-in Irish maids made the best of a very limited space, round out a most fascinating look back beyond a century.

Owned by the City of New York, the *Merchant's House Museum* is the only New York City family home preserved – inside and out – from the 19th Century, giving visitors a vivid look at how Seabury Tredwell (a successful hardware merchant), his wife Eliza and their eight children lived until their youngest daughter, Gertrude, died in 1933.

The N or R trains to 8th Street, the 6 to Astor Plaza and the B or the F to Broadway/Lafayette all leave you within walking distance of the *Merchant's House Museum*. The M5 or M6 buses to Broadway/4th Street, the M103 to 4th Street and the M1 to Broadway and 8th Street do the same.

- *MTA Today, New York City Transit Edition, 12/6/13*

Walking Distance: Astor Place; Washington Square Park; Union Square Park; Tompkins Square Park.

Morris-Jumel Mansion (MJM)

http://www.morrisjumel.org

If you happen to find yourself in the Washington Heights Section of Upper Manhattan, you may come upon a remarkable edifice, the oldest house in Manhattan, in fact.

The *Morris-Jumel Mansion (MJM)* was built by British Colonel Roger Morris in 1765. General George Washington used the mansion as his headquarters during the Battle of Harlem Heights in the fall of 1776; *President* Washington returned to *MJM* on July 10, 1790 to dine with Vice-President John Adams, Secretary of State Thomas Jefferson, Secretary of the Treasury Alexander Hamilton and Secretary of War Henry Knox.

Stephen Jumel, a prominent French wine merchant from Haiti, purchased the house in 1810. When Jumel died in 1832, he left his fortune to his wife, Eliza, who soon married again, to former Vice President Aaron Burr. Jumel divorced Burr after three years, though, and died in the mansion in 1865. The house passed through a few hands till 1894, when General Ferdinand P. Earle purchased it. He sold it in 1903 to the City of New York, in order to preserve the historical significance of the building. In 1904, the Washington's Headquarters Association, formed by four chapters of the Daughters of the American Revolution, took on the task of operating the mansion as a museum.

Located at the head of the Sylvan Terrace, which is the home of a wonderful string of old row-houses, the *Morris-Jumel* stands tall on a hill. The courtyard that surrounds the structure is open to all. Upon entering the mansion, one is struck by how loud the ancient wooden floors creak on each step you take, a sensation both thrilling and unsettling. The parlors on the first floor, the so-called "sleeping chambers" on the second floor and the basement kitchen all are well preserved and inspiring. Most of all, the idea of actually being in a house where the first three U.S Presidents had been, along with the two men involved in the most famous duel in history, Hamilton and

Burr, was rather intoxicating. And reason enough for anyone who is a New Yorker or an American to head uptown for a look at *MJM*, which became a National Landmark in 1962. There is also a wonderful gift shop in the mansion which sells items pertaining to the site as well as the colonial times it was born into.

If you take the C train to 163rd Street and exit from the southeast staircase, you'll be just a short walk from the *Morris-Jumel Mansion*, beyond a stone stairwell on St. Nicholas Avenue. The M2 and M3 buses on Madison Avenue (to 160th Street) and the Third Avenue M101 bus (to 161st Street) also stop within a few blocks of the *Mansion*.

• *MTA Today, New York City Transit Edition, 10/10/14*

Walking Distance: Trinity Cemetery; Yankee Stadium; Macombs Dam Park.

Museum of Arts & Design (MAD)

http://www.madmuseum.org

If ever the term "in the heart of" was appropriate, it is for the *Museum of Arts & Design (MAD)*, located on its own island "in the heart of" Columbus Circle, in a distinct building which looks artsy in and of itself. Having moved from its previous (smaller) home at 40 West 53rd Street in 2008, the *MAD* continues to hold the singular purpose of bringing together art, craft and design in today's world.

The nine-story building makes a concerted effort to serve the arts community in every way. The second through fifth floors contain the galleries, with permanent displays on the third level (which was, unfortunately, closed for renovations when I passed through). The sixth floor houses the Education Center, with studios available to aid in the artistic process. The seventh floor is reserved for private events, though the Atrium on the first floor and the 143-seat auditorium on the Theater (basement) level are also utilized for this purpose. There is a restaurant on the ninth floor and a gift store on the first floor.

Fashion Jewelry: The Collection of Barbara Barger, an exhibit that will run until January of 2014, took up all of the second floor gallery and contained over 450 pieces from fashion designers like Chanel, Yves St. Laurent and Dior. Barger, the daughter of a diamond merchant, acquired over 4,000 pieces of jewelry; this *MAD* representation of her collection was most impressive, even to a non-connoisseur of the craft, like me.

Two floors of the *MAD* were showing the final weeks of a most fascinating exhibit, *Against the Grain: Wood in Contemporary Art, Craft & Design*. There were various sculptures, made using different types of wood, featuring 57 artists from around the world. "*Grapes*," Chinese artist Ai Weiwei's group of Qing Dynasty (1644-1911) bar stools melded together in mid-air was probably the most interesting piece, while a giant (oak) rubber stamp, which carried the phrase "*Who is the True Terrorist?*," from Bartolemy Toguo of Cameroon, was the piece that held me strangely transfixed. Two upcoming exhibits, *Body & Soul: New International Ceramics* and *Out of Hand: Materializing the Postdigital*, look to further enhance *MAD*'s appeal to the true lover of arts, crafts and designs.

The 1, A, B, and C trains to 59th Street/Columbus Circle deliver you right outside the *Museum of Arts & Design*. The N, Q or R to 57th Street and 7th Avenue and the F to 57th Street and 5th Avenue each leave you a few blocks away. The M5, M7, M10, M20, M30 and M104 buses all stop at either Columbus Circle and 59th Street or 57th Street and 8th Avenue.

- *MTA Today, New York City Transit Edition, 10/4/13*

Walking Distance: Lincoln Center; Avery Fisher Hall; Central Park West & South; Columbus Circle; New York City Center; Carnegie Deli; Stage Deli; Carnegie Hall; Broadway Theater District.

Museum of Jewish Heritage

Of the many museums and landmarks that can be found at the southern tip of Manhattan, the *Museum of Jewish Heritage* is arguably the most unique. Combining history with the personal and religious beliefs of a very proud group of people, this wonderful structure on the banks of the Hudson (symbolically overlooking Ellis Island and the Statue of Liberty) takes one on a thought-inspiring ride through an often troubled, but always hopeful journey.

The main building consists of three floors, which collectively form a timeline to the lives of Jewish people from 1880 to the present. As the entrance to the museum states, the *Museum of Jewish Heritage* is *"A Living Memorial to the Holocaust,"* and it is with that in mind that the second floor (*"The War Against the Jews: 1930-1945"*) tells the most powerful tale. The years leading up to World War II, with the rise of Hitler and the ensuing calculated extinction of the Jewish population, are brought alive graphically. The *Holocaust* and the desperate attempts of Jews to flee Germany (mostly unsuccessful) are equally compelling, while the ultimate downfall of the Nazis by 1945 serves to preface the third floor of the museum (*"Jewish Renewal: 1945-Present"*), where the world of Jewish people from 1945 to now offered up new perspectives that I for one had not thought of so deeply before my visit.

On the first floor (*"Jewish Life a Century Ago: 1880-1930"*), the depiction of Jewish culture from 1880-1930 gave you a more defined look into how the prejudices and unfounded fears of others had hovered over the Jews of the late 19th and early 20th Centuries. Overall, the use of a timeline made the *Museum of the Jewish Heritage* much easier to grasp and understand, especially to someone from a different background.

Two special exhibits: *"Hava Nagila: A Song for the People"* and *"Against the Odds; American Jews and the Rescue of Europe's Refugees: 1933—1941,"* found in separate galleries on the third floor, helped round out an extremely insightful museum. I was particularly touched by a 1939 letter in the *"Against the Odds"* exhibit, written by renowned scientist Albert Einstein to First Lady Eleanor Roosevelt, seeking help in getting Jews safe passage to America. Overall, the *Museum of Jewish Heritage* was a very eye-opening venue.

The 4 and 5 trains to Bowling Green, the R train to Whitehall Street, the 1 to Rector Street and the M5 and M15 buses to South Ferry all leave you within walking distance of the *Museum of Jewish Heritage*. The M20 bus to Battery Park City leaves you right in front of the building.

- *MTA Today, New York City Transit Edition, 7/5/13*

Walking Distance: Skyscraper Museum; National Museum of the American Indian/New York; Battery Park; New York Korean War Veterans Memorial; Statue of Liberty/Ellis Island Ferry; Staten Island Ferry; Canyon of Heroes.

Museum of Modern Art (MoMA)

http://www.moma.org

Though I personally aspire to visit as many smaller, lesser known and hidden treasure museums in New York City in my lifetime, the thought to drop by one of the more famous ones naturally enters my soul from time to time. One of the most (rightfully) heralded museums in *The City* and in fact, the world, is the *Museum of Modern Art* or simply, the *MoMA*. This past Summer, I dropped by to see a particular exhibit, but was reminded on my trip how much the *MoMA* held within its walls.

Located in the heart of Midtown Manhattan at 11 West 53rd Street (between 5th and 6th Avenues), the *Museum of Modern Art* offers up six floors of varying and changing exhibits, a pair of theatres, three classrooms, an education center, three restaurant/cafes and the *MoMA* Design and Book store, which features a large array of art reproductions and over 2,000 book titles. When you go through the *MoMA*, both the quantity and the quality of the different forms of art on display is almost overwhelming – but well worth slowing down to examine.

The *MoMA* was first conceived in 1929, by Abby Aldrich Rockefeller (the wife of John D. Rockefeller Jr.) and two friends, Lillie P. Bliss and Mary Quinn Sullivan. The museum opened at its original site on 57th Street and 5th Avenue on November 7, 1929, nine days after the *Wall Street Crash*. Six rooms of galleries and offices made up the *MoMA* back then, with a collection of Vincent Van Gogh's work (including sixty-six oil paintings and fifty drawings), which opened on November 4, 1935, the most noted exhibit. When Abby's son Nelson became the museum's president in 1939, he soon moved the *MoMA* to its current site on 53rd Street.

I arrived at the *MoMA* one Saturday early last Summer to see work originally done on site by the Mexican muralist Diego Rivera, for the second ever single artist exhibition at the *MoMA,* which ran from December 22, 1931 to January 27, 1932. (The first featured

Henri Matisse.) The murals essentially portrayed class inequity or revolution. They were fabulous. After checking out Rivera's work, I went throughout the *MoMA* and became constantly inspired, with the *Sculpture Garden* on the first floor a particularly favorite spot. The *MoMA* holdings include over 150,000 pieces, around 22,000 films and 4 Million film stills. Among the current exhibits are *Tokyo, 1955-1970: A New Avant Garde* (through 2/25) *Inventing Abstraction, 1910-1925* (through 4/15) and *Edward Munch: The Scream* (through 4/29).

You can reach the *MoMA* by taking the E or the M train to the Lexington Avenue and 53rd Street stop.

- ***MTA Today, New York City Transit Edition, 2/26/13***

Walking Distance: Carnegie Hall; Broadway Theater District; Carnegie Deli; Stage Deli; Radio City Music Hall; Rockefeller Center; Top of the Rock Observation Deck.

Museum of the City of New York (MCNY)

http://www.mcny.org

Of all the fabulous New York museums, one of my absolute favorites is the *Museum of the City of New York (MCNY)*, which deals exclusively with the history of New York, including the people, places and things that have made this the greatest city in the world. Located on 103rd Street and 5th Avenue, the *Museum of the City of New York* takes you on a ride through the very heart of New York, past, present and (presumably) future.

Founded in 1923 as a private non-profit corporation, the *MCNY* celebrates New York's tradition of diversity, tracks the constantly changing landscape and attempts to interpret the character of *The City*. I had been there once when I was very young, but had not returned until a few years ago, when I went to see a new exhibit entitled: *The Glory Days of New York Baseball: 1947-1957*, which included photos, videos and priceless artifacts from the final seasons in which New York was the home of three baseball teams: the Yankees, the Giants and the Brooklyn Dodgers. This fit right into the fabric of the various other New York exhibits in the museum at the time and reminded me what a fabulous venue the *MCNY* was. The many photos and artifacts from *The Glory Days of New York Baseball: 1947-1957* have been preserved in an excellent online exhibit on the museum's website.

Going back to the museum recently, I was instantly conscious of an upgrade in the building, which now seemed larger and more accessible. Current exhibits, like *Making Room: New Models for Housing New Yorkers,* which used wooden models to show new ideas for housing in *The City* and *Currier & Ives and other Winter Tales*, which featured Winter-themed paintings of Washington Square, Central Park and other venues in the 19th Century, were particularly powerful. *Timescapes: A Multimedia Portrait of New York,* a 25-minute documentary that plays at 15 minutes and 45 minutes after the hour, provided a great time capsule of the history of New York from 1609-present. *Activist New York*, though, was probably my favorite exhibit, the one all New Yorkers should go and see. And as you get off the elevator on the third floor, there is an absolutely spectacular (and huge) painting of the present day Grand Central Station, which would be reason enough to go to the *MCNY*.

The M1, M3, M4 or M106 buses to 104th Street or the M2 bus to 101st Street all leave you right near the *Museum of the City of New York*. The 6 train to 103rd Street or the 2 and 3 trains to Central Park North/110th Street also leave you just a few blocks away.

- ***MTA Today, New York City Transit Edition, 5/24/13***

Walking Distance: El Museo del Barrio; Central Park Conservatory Gardens; Harlem Meer.

Museum of the Moving Image/ Kaufman Astoria Studios

http://www.ammi.org   http://www.kaufmanastoria.com

Located just a few subway stops from Manhattan, the *Museum of the Moving Image* (*MMI*), which opened in 1988, is a most unique venue, one of thirteen buildings within an historic Queens complex, which also includes the *Kaufman Astoria Studios* and a multiplex movie theatre. The only museum in the United States dedicated to exploring the art, history and technology of the moving image, the museum and its adjoining buildings were built on the site of the original *Astoria Studios*, which was opened in 1920 by the Famous Players-Lasky Corporation and served as Paramount's East Coast headquarters in the mid-20's and beyond. Hundreds of silent and early sound Era movies were made there, including the first two Marx Brothers movies, *The Cocoanuts* (1929) and *Animal Crackers* (1930). In 1942, the US Army took over the studios to produce training films for WWII servicemen, before maintaining the complex for a few decades. In the 1970's, the studios were abandoned, until 1980, when real estate developer George Kaufman was chosen to operate the studio facilities. The *Astoria Motion Picture and Television Center Foundation* had been established in 1977 to restore the *Astoria Studio* complex to productive use for all types of films. In addition, TV shows starring Bill Cosby, Dan Aykroyd and Whoopi Goldberg have all called the refurbished *Kaufman Astoria Studios* home in the past two decades.

Rochelle Slovin, the Executive Director of the *Foundation,* led the way to creating a museum of film and television in one of the complex's buildings. This became the *MMI*, which was originally called the *American Museum of the Moving* image. Today, the *MMI*, the *Kaufman Astoria Studios* and the *United Artists Theatres* (which consists of 14 theatres) form the core of the complex.

The central exhibit in the MMI, "*Behind the Screen,*" uses parts of two floors of the museum to show all aspects (producing, promoting, presenting) of how images come alive on TV, movie or other electronic media screens. Admission to the *MMI* includes access to the various genres of movies which are screened on a daily basis, while some screenings (which often include special celebrity guests) require tickets which can be bought online. Currently, *Showtime's* "Nurse Jackie" and the children's favorite, "Sesame Street," occupy studio space at *Kaufman*. A working back lot is currently being constructed on a one-block area outside the studios, which should make the *Kaufman Astoria Studios* even more alluring to all sorts of filmmakers.

The Steinway Street station on the M and R trains and the 36th Avenue station on the N or Q trains leave you within walking distance of the *Museum of the Moving Image*, which is closed on Mondays and Tuesdays.

- *MTA Today, New York City Transit Edition, 4/19/13*

Walking Distance: Steinway Street Business Improvement District; Sunnyside; Long Island City.

National Academy Museum

http://www.nationalacademy.org

Some of the most interesting museums in *The City* are highly understated. A great example of this is the *National Academy Museum*, which stands across the street from the famous *Guggenheim* on 89th Street and Fifth Avenue. The *Grand Academy* is an almost hidden jewel, standing right in plain sight, in the building it has occupied since 1942.

The *National Academy* was formed in 1825 by a group of artists, among them Rembrandt Peale and Thomas Cole. Their goal was to mirror the *Royal Academy* in London, in the hopes of promoting fine arts in the United States, through both exhibition and instruction. The founders of the *Academy* felt that art could flourish in this country beyond the parameters of the usual aristocratic patronage system. For the first four decades of the *National Academy's* existence, various sites along Broadway and on Chambers Street were used for exhibitions.

In 1860, a site on 23rd Street and Fourth Avenue (now Park Avenue South) was purchased to build the *Academy* a permanent home. The *National Academy Building*, designed by Peter B. Wight, opened in 1865, with a school, exhibition space and offices on the grounds. In 1899, the building was sold to the Metropolitan Life Insurance Company. The exhibitions of the *Academy* again vagabonded into the 1940's, while their school was located at 109th Street and Amsterdam Avenue. During this period, annual exhibitions were held in the galleries of the *American Fine Arts Society.*

The current site was realized in 1942, along what was then known as Millionaires Row (now *Museum Mile*), in a mansion originally owned by Archer Milton Huntington (1870-1955) and his wife, sculptor Anna Hyatt Huntington (1876-1973). Huntington, the heir to the fortune of his father, Collis, an owner of the Central Pacific and Southern Pacific railroads, is best known as the founder of the *Hispanic Society* in New York City. His mansion would prove more than adequate to house the *National Academy Museum and School* into the 21st Century.

Today, the recently (2011) renovated museum offers three floors of galleries, which draw from the vast collection of almost two centuries, as well as the present. The school, which has thrived on all aspects of art, from sketching to live model drawing and other studio-based study, is one of the most revered art schools in the United States. There is no admission required to view the *National Academy Museum*; one can donate whatever they choose to on the way out.

The 6 train to 86th Street leaves you a few blocks from the *National Academy Museum*. The M1, M2, M3 or M4 buses on Fifth and Madison Avenues to 89th Street do the same.

- ***MTA Today, New York City Transit Edition, 11/14/14***

<u>Walking Distance</u>: Solomon R. Guggenheim Museum; Neue Gallerie New York; Metropolitan Museum of Art; Cooper Hewitt, Smithsonian Design Museum; Jewish Museum; Ukrainian Institute of America.

National Museum of the American Indian/New York

http://nmai.si.edu/home

As New Yorkers, we are lost at times to the wealth of museums, parks and other places of interest to see. As Transit workers, many of us roam *The City* purposefully, yet miss fabulous places along the way. For those of us who work at 2 Broadway, the greatest example of this may well be the *National Museum of the American Indian*, which is located right across the street, at 1 Bowling Green. Residing on two floors of the Historic Alexander Hamilton U.S. Customs Building, the *NMAI* in the *George Gustav Heye Center* offers up one of the most complete revolving collections of Native American art, sculpture and history. It is one of three facilities that make up the *National Museum of the American Indian*, the others being in the *National Mall* in Washington, D.C and in Suitland, Maryland, which houses *The Cultural Resources Center*. Where once the duty collections of the Port of New York passed through these walls, now the tale of the true Americans and how they survived, endured and thrived, despite having been treated in an often unspeakable way through the generations, is told.

The *National Museum of the American Indian* was established in 1989, with the three sites offering up some 800,000 artifacts, as well as over 125,000 photographic images. At the Customs House in New York, the most prominent permanent exhibition is the *"Infinity of Nations: Art and History in the Collections of the National Museum of the American Indian."* Current traveling exhibitions include *"Julie Buffalohead: Let the Show Begin"* (through April 28), *"C. Maxx Stevens: House of Memories"* (through June 16) and *"Up Where We Belong: Native Musicians in Popular Culture"* (through August 11).

A lunch hour's walk through the *Museum's* halls gives you a sense of the customs and the lifestyle that have served the American Indians well for centuries. Minnesota architect Cass Gilbert designed the building in the Beaux-Arts style in 1902-07. This architecture, fine arts and engineering mix still holds up today and gives the entrance hall to *NMAI* a most lavish feel. A fine bookstore/gift shop offers up a diverse collection of Native American crafts and reading material. Admission is free, so there is no good reason for anyone who works in Downtown Manhattan to miss this unique and informative museum. (I try to go at least once a year.) And for anyone else looking for an uplifting experience, the *NMAI* is located in an easily accessible area.

The 4 or 5 train to Bowling Green, the R train to Whitehall Street, the 1 train to Rector Street and the 2 or the 3 line to Wall Street leave you right in front of or a few blocks from the *National Museum of the American Indian*. The M5, M15 and M20 buses also drop you off right outside the museum.

- *MTA Today, New York City Transit Edition, 3/6/13*

Walking Distance: Skyscraper Museum; Museum of Jewish Heritage; Battery Park; New York Korean War Veterans Memorial; Statue of Liberty/Ellis Island Ferry; Staten Island Ferry; Canyon of Heroes.

New-York Historical Society Museum & Library

http://www.nyhistory.org

Located at 77th Street and Central Park West, the *New-York Historical Society Museum & Library* is the oldest museum in the City of New York, pre-dating The Metropolitan Museum of Art by almost seventy years. Opening in 1804 and currently holding over 1.6 million items, including a robust collection of portraits and all 435 existing watercolors of John James Audubon's seminal work, *Birds of America*, the museum boasts a truly amazing collection. The *New-York Historical Society's Patricia D. Klingenstein Library* contains more than three million books, pamphlets, maps, atlases, newspapers, music sheets, manuscripts, prints, photographs and architectural drawings. One of only sixteen libraries in the United States qualified to be a member of the Independent Research Libraries Association, the *Klingenstein Library* features a vast range of Civil War material, including U.S. Grant's terms of surrender for Robert E. Lee.

Statues of Abraham Lincoln and Frederick Douglass at the museum's two entrances greet visitors, before heading into a most inspiring array of halls. On the main floor (every half hour), they screen a wonderful short film called *"New York Story,"* which gives a condensed (yet filling) timeline of New York City's rich history, from Dutch trading port to cultural center of the world. On my visit, exhibits like *"Swing Time: Reginald March and Thirties New York"* and *"Aids in New York; The First Five Years"* were riveting. Upcoming displays, like *"The Armory Show at 100: Modern Art and Revolution,"* promise to similarly spur the imagination. Beyond the various revolving exhibitions is *The Luce Center* on the top floor of the *NYHS*. There you will find an astonishing collection of over 40,000 items, presented on a two-tiered ongoing display, featuring paintings, sculptures, coins, ribbons, ceramics, metals, glassware and more, with an 18th Century traveling coach right at the center of it all. If you only ventured into the *New-York Historical Society Museum* for a tour of *The Luce Center*, you would leave visibly satisfied.

Ongoing Children's Programs like *The Civil War in 50 Objects Family Scavenger Hunt* and *Macy's Sunday Story Time*, along with the *DiMenna Children's History Museum* (which shows New York through the eyes of children from the past 300 years), add a unique touch to the goings on at the *NYHS*. There are also lectures continuously scheduled on the calendar. (*The Distinguished Speakers Series* is a staple.) The museum's galleries are closed on Mondays and the *Klingenstein Library* is closed on Sunday and Monday.

The B and C trains to 81st Street and the 1 train to 79th Street leave you right by the *New-York Historical Society Museum & Library*, located at 170 Central Park West.

- ***MTA Today, New York City Transit Edition, 1/3/14***

<u>Walking Distance</u>: American Museum of Natural History; Central Park West; Beacon Theater; American Folk Art Museum; 79th Street Boat Basin.

Queens Museum

http://www.queensmuseum.org

In early November of 2013, there was a grand re-opening in an area where millions once came in the present to see the prospective future. The last World's Fair held in New York, in 1964-65, left behind a few remnants of that dramatic time. The iconic *Unisphere*, the symbol of that Fair, still stands, as does a newer, more elaborate and exciting *Hall of Science*. And then there is the *Queens Museum*, which (among other exhibits) is most famous for the *Panorama of the City of New York*, an almost inconceivable scale model of New York City.

Built for the 1939-40 New York World's Fair, what was originally called the *New York City Building* housed the *New York Pavilion*, which featured displays about municipal agencies. Centrally located at the Flushing, Queens site, it was one of the only buildings that remained for permanent usage after the Fair closed in 1940, when it became a recreation area, including a roller rink and an ice rink, in the newly developed Flushing Meadows-Corona Park. Today, it is the only surviving building from the 1939-40 World's Fair. From 1946-50, the rinks were covered, as the *New York City Building* became the home of the United Nations General Assembly, while the UN's permanent home was being completed in Manhattan. When the United Nations left, the rinks were re-opened.

In preparation for the 1964-65 World's Fair, the building was again slated to become the Fair's *New York Pavilion*, with a fabulous display called the *Panorama of the City of New York* added. This scale model, which survived the 1964-65 Fair and saw many updates added through the years, remained a unique exhibit, wherein every building in all five boroughs is represented. The ice rink returned in the South side of the building, while the roller rink on the North side was superseded by the *Panorama* and, in 1972, the *Queens Center for Art and Culture*, which incorporated the *Panorama* as a permanent exhibit. The building would be known as the *Queens Museum of Art* for the next four decades.

In November of 2013, following another renovation, which included the elimination of the ice rink area back into the original building, the newly named *Queens Museum* re-opened as a brand new art venue, whose 105,000 square feet doubled the size of its predecessor. Exhibits featuring the World's Fairs that were once held here and the enduring *Panorama* are still the highlights of this modest, yet effective two-story museum.

To reach the *Queens Museum*, take the 7 train to the Mets-Willets Point station and walk into Flushing Meadows-Corona Park, where you can follow the signs, or simply head toward the *Unisphere*, which stands right outside the museum.

- *MTA Today, New York City Transit Edition, 8/1/14*

Walking Distance: USTA Billie Jean King National Tennis Center; Terrace on the Park; New York Hall of Science; Queens Zoo; Citi Field.

Skyscraper Museum

http://www.skyscraper.org/home.htm

Just across the street from the *Museum of Jewish Heritage* is another rather distinct museum, the *Skyscraper Museum*. Set inside the building at 36 Battery Place, this look at the evolution of vertical art and construction is most properly located in New York City. With images of just about every tall building that's gone up in the last few centuries, plus models of a few of the more current and/or famous ones to view, the *Skyscraper Museum* attempts, mostly with success, to tell the tale of the concrete cloud busters, past and present.

The museum itself is modest, merely taking up a piece of the second floor of the building, though mirrored ceilings give the illusion of height, a most representative element for a venue such as this. The main exhibit currently on display chronicles the history of the *Woolworth Building*, the iconic structure at 233 Broadway which is celebrating its 100th birthday in 2013. From the time when it opened on April 24, 1913 until 1930, the *Woolworth* was the tallest building in the world. (*40 Wall Street*, then the *Chrysler Building* and ultimately the *Empire State Building* came along in succession in 1930-31 to take the tallest building "title.") As the current linchpin of the collection, plans, drawings, models and extensive media write-ups of and about the *Woolworth Building* look to take up a good portion of the *Skyscraper Museum* for the rest of the year.

Naturally, the nearby goings on in Downtown Manhattan made it almost mandatory that a section of the museum told the tale of the *World Trade Center* and the new building currently rising through the sky where the original stood, before the attacks of September 11, 2001. But there are also photos and models of various famous tall buildings, like the Sears Tower in Chicago, the Petronas Towers in Kuala Lumpur and the Burj Khalifa in Dubai, currently the tallest building in the world at 2,722 feet. My only issue with the museum is that the Empire State Building didn't have enough representation (at this time) to my liking.

The *Skyscraper Museum* can be easily traversed in a lunch hour and can also be a very solid part of a really interesting day, if visited collectively with a few of the other museums in the Battery Park area

The 4 and 5 trains to Bowling Green, the R train to Whitehall Street, the 1 train to Rector Street and the M5 and M15 buses to South Ferry all leave you within walking distance of the *Skyscraper Museum*. The M20 bus to Battery Park City leaves you right in front of the building.

- *MTA Today, New York City Transit Edition, 7/12/13*

<u>**Walking Distance**</u>: Museum of Jewish Heritage; National Museum of the American Indian/New York; Battery Park; New York Korean War Veterans Memorial; Statue of Liberty/Ellis Island Ferry; Staten Island Ferry; Canyon of Heroes.

Solomon R. Guggenheim Museum

http://www.guggenheim.org

One of the most recognizable museums in the world, due to the building design by the legendary architect Frank Lloyd Wright, the *Solomon R. Guggenheim Museum* is another wonderful venue to visit along the celebrated "Museum Mile" on Fifth Avenue, across from Central Park. Located between 88th and 89th Streets, *The Guggenheim*, with its cascading white spirals rising skyward to signify its uniqueness, does, in a way, provide one with a most different viewing experience. For as you peruse the particular main exhibit which is on display, your clockwise circular walk, though it does not leave you dizzy, certainly gives you a sense of the journey that the artists took to get to where they were going.

First established at 25 East 54th street as the *Museum of Non-Objective Painting* by the Solomon R. Guggenheim Foundation in 1939, the organization took on its current name in 1952, upon the death of its founder. As for the iconic current building's history, in June of 1943, Guggenheim's art advisor, Hilla Rebay, asked Frank Lloyd Wright to design a building to house the four-year old *Museum of Non-Objective Painting.* Various disagreements over the museum's site (Wright didn't favor New York City) and design left the project in limbo for years. As it turned our both Guggenheim and Wright would both die before October 21, 1959, when the cylindrical building, wider at the top than the bottom, opened at 1071 Fifth Avenue. *The Guggenheim* has since been hailed as one of the greatest architectural achievements of the 20th Century. Two expansions, in 1992 (when a second tower was built) and 2005-2008, further enhanced the appeal of *The Guggenheim.*

Some have felt that the building's outer presence would overshadow the art in the museum itself, but Wright thought otherwise, that in fact, this design would accentuate the art in its environs. In any case, *The Guggenheim* remains, to this day, one of the most recognizable and interesting museums in New York, if not the world. The six rotunda levels and seven annex levels make for a satisfying afternoon of viewing. Vasily Kandinsky (1866-1944) a Moscow born artist whose work Guggenheim had amassed a large collection of, is still a staple at *The Guggenheim.* A pair of restaurants on the first and third levels can provide visitors a brief respite. The *Peter B. Lewis Theater* on the first floor provides regular screenings.

To get to *The Guggenheim*, take the 6 train to 86th street and walk up to 5th Avenue and 88th street. To reach the museum by bus, take the M1, M2, M3, or M4 bus on Madison or Fifth Avenue.

- **MTA Today, New York City Transit Edition, 9/12/14**

Walking Distance: National Academy Museum; The Metropolitan Museum of Art; Neue Gallery New York; Cooper-Hewitt National Design Museum; Ukranian Institute of America; Jewish Museum.

The Anne Frank Center USA

http://annefrank.com

A block off Broadway and City Hall Park, a small, yet significant mini-museum shares one of the great stories of resilience and humanity ever told. The *Anne Frank Center USA*, located at 44 Park Place, is a short ride through an interminable two-year period in which eight human beings hid out in a "Secret Annex," from the Nazi occupation in Amsterdam. The story of Anne Frank, brought alive in the pages of the world renowned book, *"Anne Frank: Diary of a Young Girl,"* has lost none of its luster or emotion, more than half a century since it was first published by her father, Otto Frank, the lone annex survivor of the *Holocaust*. This museum, which can be mistaken for a generic storefront if one walks by too quickly, effectively uses a limited space to bring alive the story of hope in the words of a teenage girl of the 1940's. The amount of information and history contained in the modest *Anne Frank Center USA* forms a perfect analogy to how those living in an equally small area somehow managed to survive.

At the front desk you are met by museum custodians who will gladly walk you through the two rooms that make up the *Center*, or let you survey the exhibits on your own. There is a short documentary that can be cued up at any time for visitors, which gives a brief overview of the time, the place and the plight of Anne Frank, her parents, Otto and Edith, her older sister Margot, Hermann and Auguste Van Pels, their son Peter and Fritz Pfeffer. A scale model shows the layout of the attic where they hid from July of 1942 until August of 1944, when Nazi soldiers broke into the Annex by removing the bookshelf which covered the secret entrance. I thought I had some sense of the scope of the attic, but I have to say that this model gave me a new and (obviously) clearer perspective on the entire extraordinary tale.

There are timelines on the fates of all those who hid for the two years, as well as those who helped hide them, including the remarkable Miep Gies, Otto Frank's assistant (who salvaged Anne's diary and lived to be 100). The spirit of hope and perseverance in the face of an unimaginable evil comes alive in this serene setting, ironically located just a short walk from where another of the world's greatest inhumanities occurred on September 11, 2001.

The R train to City Hall, the A or C to Chambers Street, the 2 or 3 to Park Place and the 4 or 5 to Fulton Street all leave you a short walk away, while the final stop on the E train (World Trade Center) leaves you right across the street.

- *MTA Today, New York City Transit Edition, 1/25/12*

<u>Walking Distance</u>: City Hall Park; 9/11 Memorial & Museum; Canyon of Heroes; Irish Hunger Memorial.

The Drawing Center

http://www.drawingcenter.org

As anyone even vaguely familiar with the *SoHo* area knows, this is a special place within *The City* which gravitates toward and is replete with artists, writers and other creative types. Amongst all the kinetic energy which has defined *SoHo* for over a Century, there are certain venues that hold a special place to the artistic community, locally, nationally and abroad. One of these is *The Drawing Center*.

The Drawing Center is the only fine arts institution in the U.S. to focus solely on the exhibition of drawings, both historical and contemporary. Located at 35 Wooster Street, just off Canal Street, it was established in 1977 to provide opportunities for emerging and under-recognized artists, to demonstrate the significance and diversity of drawings throughout history and to stimulate public dialogue on issues of art and culture. An acclaimed "small" museum, *The Drawing Center* gives an intimate and close-up view of a variety of artists and how drawing connects to other creative entities like science, literature, architecture, theater and film. There is a regular turnover of disparate works on display, which accentuates the notion of drawing as a vibrant creative catalyst. There are over 1,500 emerging artists on *The Drawing Center's* curated Artists' Registry.

The Drawing Center has an interesting program called the Drawing Papers, which are essentially records of each exhibit that passes through, which are then bound into a chronologically numbered catalogues. The *"Thread Lines'* catalog that I purchased (#118) gave me a traveling record of all that I'd seen of that particular sewing/weaving/knitting exhibit, including the threaded "minims' of Shelia Hicks and Jessica Rankin's lunar orb-inspired *"Termagant."* Live performance artists are also often in the mix at *The Drawing Center*, helping make it a most thought-provoking spot to visit.

As an educational entity, *The Drawing Center's* Edward Hallam Tuck Publication Program, the previously noted Drawing Papers publication series and a lively array of Public Programs (panel discussions, concerts, family art workshops, etc.) help connect the public more deeply with the works on display. In addition, *The Drawing Center's* Michael Iovenko School Programs have served 75,000 local public school students through drawing activities and discussions inspired by the approaches of artists currently on display. An Internship Program has also introduced hundreds of college students to the workings of a vibrant and evolving museum.

If you take the J, N, Q, R or 6 trains to Canal Street, a short walk West to Wooster Street and a right turn brings you a block and a half from *The Drawing Center.* If you take the A, C, E or 1 trains to Canal Street, a short walk East and a left turn does the same.

• *MTA Today, New York City Transit Edition, 12/5/14*

<u>Walking Distance</u>: New York City Fire Museum; Ward-Nasse Gallery; Canal Street Shopping District.

The Metropolitan Museum of Art (The Met)

www.metmuseum.org/en

One of the most famous museums in the City of New York (or the world, for that matter) is the *Metropolitan Museum of Art*, or *The Met*, as it is universally known. Located on 5ᵗʰ Avenue and 82ⁿᵈ Street since March 30, 1880, *The Met* has seen many additions and modifications made to the main building since as early as 1888, with renovations in 2014 to the four-block Plaza on Fifth Avenue the latest.

The Metropolitan Museum of Art dates back to 1866, when a group of Americans agreed to create a "National institution and gallery of art" for the American people. The idea, proposed by lawyer John Jay, came to fruition on April 13, 1870, when *The Met* was incorporated and opened to the public in the Dodworth Building at 681 Fifth Avenue. After a brief layover at the Douglas Mansion at 128 West 14ᵗʰ Street, *The Met* moved to its current location, where it has become the largest art museum in the United States and one of the ten largest on the planet.

Today, *The Metropolitan Museum of Art's* main building offers one of the most significant art collections in the world. Along with its smaller location uptown, *The Cloisters*, which houses medieval art, *The Met* has a collection of over 2 million works of art. On 82ⁿᵈ and Fifth, the pure volume of these works is staggering, to say the least. Paintings, sculptures and other artifacts from the Greeks, Egyptians and Romans highlight a vast collection of European art and the fabulous *American Wing* is an obvious favorite. The *Robert Lehman Collection*, donated by the estate of the banker upon his death, displays one of the largest personal art collections known to man. The *Arms and Armor* section on the first floor is another popular area at *The Met*, but there is truly something in this venue to excite, inspire or intrigue just about anyone.

The renovation of the Plaza outside *The Met* will include contemporary fountains, trees and aerial hedges, as well as more seating for the public and enhanced lighting, to illuminate *The Met's* familiar façade at night. *The Met* also sponsors and/or moderates many special events, including concerts, readings and lectures. There are also guided tours of the different galleries available daily, as well as a "museum highlights" tour. Overall, *The Met* is one of the true jewels of *The City*.

To get to *The Met*, take the 4, 5 or 6 trains to 86th street and walk three blocks west to the 5th Avenue entrance on 82nd Street. Or take the M1, M2, M3 and M4 buses along 5th Avenue (uptown) to 82nd Street and Madison Avenue (downtown) to 83rd Street.

- ***MTA Today, New York City Transit Edition, 6/14/14***

Walking Distance: National Academy Museum; Solomon R. Guggenheim Museum; Neue Gallery New York; Cooper-Hewitt National Design Museum; Ukranian Institute of America; Whitney Museum of Art

The Morgan Library & Museum

http://www.themorgan.org/home.asp

In 1906, legendary American financier J. Pierpont Morgan had a library built adjacent to his home on 36th Street and Madison Avenue, to house his vast number of literary and historical manuscripts, books, master drawings and prints. In 1924, 11 years after Morgan's death, his son, J.P. Morgan, Jr., fulfilled a wish his father had by making the library a public institution. Over the years, the resultant library and museum expanded on a number of occasions, with purchases and donations of rare musical manuscripts, early children's books and various items from the 19th and 20th Centuries added to the original collection. Today, *The Morgan Library & Museum* is a complex of interconnected rooms based at 225 Madison Avenue at 36th Street.

The museum part of *The Morgan*, as it is called, consisted of three galleries. One was showing *Illuminating Faith: The Eucharist in Medieval Life and Art,* another featured *Subliming Vessel: The Drawings of Matthew Barney* (a contemporary artist) and the third offered *Old Masters, Newly Acquired*, which held 19th Century artwork, including pieces by French artists Cezanne, Monet and Renoir. An upcoming exhibition entitled *Edgar Allan Poe: Terror of the Soul* will doubtless find me back at the halls of *The Morgan* very soon. The museum galleries were all very impressive, but it was the *Morgan's Library* that was truly inspiring.

Each of the three rooms of *Pierpont Morgan's Library* still maintain a magical feel, over 100 years after the *Library* was dedicated. *The East Room*, which was the *Original Library*, contained the most books and manuscripts, including a 19th Century 8-volume *Dictionary of Painters & Engravers* and one full wall dedicated to Bibles of all sizes, in various languages. *The North Room*, which was the office of Morgan's librarian, Belle DeCosta Greene, held letters from Jane Austen and Albert Einstein, among other treasures. And *The West Room*, Morgan's personal study, featured a vaulted area, open today so that visitors could get a glimpse of where Morgan's most treasured books and manuscripts were stored. A glorious Rotunda just outside the *Library* held a high school essay on "Napoleon," written by Morgan in 1854 and a 1911 editorial cartoon called "The Magnet," which depicted Morgan acquiring pieces of art by using a giant magnet. All in all, *The Morgan* was an extremely fascinating place.

The 6 train to 33rd Street, the 4, 5, 6, or 7 to Grand Central and the B, D, F, M, N, Q or R to 34th Street/Herald Square all leave you within walking distance of *The Morgan Library & Museum*. The M2, M3, M4 and Q 32 buses to 36th Street all leave you right outside.

- *MTA Today, New York City Transit Edition, 9/27/13*

Walking Distance: International Center of Photography; Empire State Building; Bryant Park; New York Public Library; Grand Central Terminal; Times Square.

The Museum of American Illustration

http://www.societyillustrators.org

Located at the *Society of Illustrators* headquarters on 63rd Street, just off Lexington Avenue, *The Museum of American Illustration* presents a most unique and defined facet of artwork. The galleries and exhibits found in this five-story townhouse, which was originally a carriage house built in 1875 for financier J.P. Morgan's personal secretary, William P. Read, are variously eye-opening, inspiring and just plain interesting.

The *Society of Illustrators*, which was founded in 1901 by nine artists and one businessman, bought the property at 128 East 63rd Street in 1939 with funds raised from the sale of their "Illustrator Show" skits (to the Schubert Organization, for the Broadway hit, "Artists and Models"). A street-level gallery opened in the 1950's, with renovations following in 1968. In 1981, *Society* President John Witt headed a campaign that formed *The Museum of American Illustration*, with a second gallery added for display to the general public. Today, the *Society of Illustrators* consists of three floors of galleries, and also hosts lectures, competitions and other drawing opportunities for professionals and students.

An exhibit entitled *Maurice Sendak: A Celebration of the Artist and His Work*, currently occupies two floors of this modest, yet rich museum. Over 200 originals by Sendak, whose work has appeared in children's books, poster illustrations and theater designs, offer a fascinating look at his craft. In 1963, the book *Where the Wild Things Are* brought Sendak's images their greatest forum. The bottom floor of *The Museum of American illustration* is dedicated entirely to the 50th Anniversary of his "Wild Things," creatures most of us have seen in our lifetime or our children's, even if we did not know the name of the illustrator. Throughout the Sendak exhibit, many original pencil drawings are matted alongside the water-colored, completed items, giving one a taste of the artist's sensibilities.

On the third floor, the Members Gallery celebrates *"The Art of Eric Fowler,"* an artist who has documented everyday life for over a quarter of a century, and in the Hall of Fame Gallery, *"Henry Patrick Raleigh: A Giant from the Era of the Golden Age of American Illustration"* offers up works that span the years 1900-1930. All three exhibits run through August 17th. A representative book/souvenir store is at the entrance of the building and there are regular "Sketch Nights" on Tuesdays and Thursdays, where aspiring artists can hone their craft. The museum is free, but I had no qualms about dropping a Lincoln into the donations box at the entranceway.

The M98, M101, M102, and M103 buses (running along Lexington Avenue), the Q32 (running along 60th Street) and the N, R, 4, 5 and 6 trains to 59th Street/Lexington Avenue all leave you within walking distance of the *Museum of American Illustration.*

- *MTA Today, New York City Transit Edition, 8/16/12*

<u>Walking Distance</u>: Central Park Zoo; FAO Schwarz; 107th Infantry Memorial; Asia Society & Museum.

The New York City Fire Museum

http://www.nycfiremuseum.org

Another of the many less heralded museums in New York City is the *New York City Fire Museum*, located at 278 Spring Street in *SoHo*. I went there recently with a predetermined notion that I'd really enjoy this place, yet I could not have imagined how truly interesting and inspiring it turned out to be. The *NYC Fire Museum* consists of two floors of artifacts and a gift shop, all within a former actual firehouse.

From October 20, 1865 to April 1, 1959, when it was closed down, *Engine 30* honorably served the *SoHo* area. From 1959 to 1974, the upper floors of the firehouse were used for medical care and as a reporting site for potential new hires. The facility closed entirely in 1974 and remained abandoned for a number of years, during which time the idea for a museum to honor, celebrate and chronicle New York City fireman was broached. On October 9, 1987, the *New York City Fire Museum* was opened.

Upon entering the *Fire Museum*, you find yourself in the gift shop, with a staircase to your right that leads to the second floor exhibits. To me, the most fascinating items up there were a pair of absolutely wonderful old hand drawn hose reels that once patrolled my Astoria/Long Island City neighborhood, an 1857 model from the *Astoria Hose Company No. 8* and a similar 1875 beauty from the *Steinway Hose Company No. 7*. The oldest exhibit on the premises was a thing called the *Bolton Quickstep*, an 1820 wooden "engine" from Bolton, Massachusetts, which required at least four firefighters to operate.

On the first floor, there was another array of engines, as well as a two-room special section whose doorways were marked *"9-11-01."* Among other *9/11* artifacts, these rooms contained a model that depicted the Downtown Manhattan area before and after the Trade Center attacks, as well as how it will look in the future. There was also a sculpture which showed the images of all 343 firefighters lost on *9/11*, where I instantly migrated to the picture of Firefighter Leon Smith, Jr. of *Ladder 118* in Brooklyn, the son of a my longtime friend and Transit co-worker, Irene Smith.

Throughout the *NYC Fire Museum*, there were displays of helmets, patches and badges from various companies through the years. There was a modest statue of a firefighter saving a young girl and a number of paintings of former officials. Overall, the *New York City Fire Museum* is yet another place I think all New Yorkers should take the time to visit.

The C and E trains and the M10 and M21 buses to Spring Street all leave you right down the block from the *New York City Fire Museum.*

- *MTA Today, New York City Transit Edition, 7/19/13*

___Walking Distance:___ Children's Museum of the Arts; The Drawing Center; Ward-Nasse Gallery..

The New York City Police Museum

__www.nycpm.org__

One of the most interesting and thought-provoking museums in Manhattan is the *New York City Police Museum*, normally located at 100 Old Slip, right on the banks of the East River. As of November, 2013, the site of the *NYCPM* was still being repaired for water damage, due to Hurricane Sandy, so the boys in blue found a new, temporary home just a short walk away, courtesy of the *SWATCH* company, which donated the site at 45 Wall Street. In any case, a visit to the exhibits contained in the *Police Museum* is well worth the time for anyone even vaguely familiar with the proud history of New York City law enforcement.

The 1st Precinct moved into its new home at 100 Old Slip in 1911, in a building constructed on the same site as a previous stationhouse, there from 1884-1909. It was built in the Neo-Italian Renaissance style, with a series of tall arches the enduring visual image today. The 1st Precinct was housed here until 1973, at which time the 1st and 4th precincts were merged. As a result of the merger, the 1st Precinct name was kept but the personnel were all moved to the larger 4th Precinct stationhouse, further uptown. In December of 2001, 100 Old Slip became the new home of the *New York City Police Museum*, which had been housed, since its inception in 2000, on nearby Broadway.

Inside the *Police Museum*, there are many fabulous artifacts, such as a burglar's tool kit owned by legendary bank robber Willie Sutton and the Thompson submachine gun used by Al Capone's henchmen to kill fellow mobster Frankie Yale. The evolution of transportation in the department is highlighted by a current day police motorcycle right at the heart of the exhibit. There are uniforms from various Eras, a chronological timeline of the NYPD and a moving exhibit to the memory of those lost on 9/11. The growing role of women and minority officers is noted, as well as the far-reaching influence of men like Police Commissioner Theodore Roosevelt (1895-97), Lieutenant Joe Petrosino, a pioneering New York cop murdered in Sicily while on assignment in 1909 and Mayor Fiorello LaGuardia

(1934-45). A gift shop at the rear of the museum offers various police-related paraphernalia.

The J and Z trains to the Broad Street station leave you just a short walk to 100 Old Slip, the once and future home of *the New York City Police Museum*. The R train to Whitehall Street and the 2, 3, 4, and 5 trains to Wall Street also leave you within short walking distance. (In late 2014, the Police Museum moved out of 45 Wall Street and prepared to return to 100 Old Slip.)

- *MTA Today, New York City Transit Edition, 7/18/14*

Walking Distance: Trinity Church; Canyon of Heroes; Statue of Liberty/Ellis Island Ferry; Staten Island Ferry; National Museum of the American Indian; Museum of Jewish heritage; Skyscraper Museum; Fraunces Tavern.

The Rubin Museum of Art

http://www.rubinmuseum.org

Many of *The City's* well known and revered museums helped secure their place on the landscape by being around for a very long time. As the decades and/or the centuries turn, legacies naturally form. Every once in a while, though, a new and different venue opens, which then begins the trek of leaving its own mark. One of these recent editions to the New York cultural scene is *The Rubin Museum of Art*.

Located on 17th Street and 7th Avenue, *The Rubin*, which opened in October of 2004, is dedicated to Himalayan art, most notably works from Tibet. The focus on an eastern culture, seen mostly as mysterious in many quarters, provides a most fascinating day at the museum for anyone so inclined to drop by. Founded by Donald and Shelley F. Rubin, who began collecting Himalayan and Tibetan artworks in the 1980's, the museum's galleries come mainly from the Rubin family collection.

The Rubin contains over 2,000 works which span the 1,800 mile Himalayan mountain range, from Afghanistan in the Northwest to Burma in the Southeast. Bhutan, Nepal, Mongolia and as noted above, Tibet, are areas represented at *The Rubin*, as are India, China, Iran and Central and Southeast Asia. A trip to *The Rubin* would be a great companion piece to a visit to the further Uptown *Asia Society*. The permanent Rubin family collection is enhanced by numerous changing exhibitions, while important worldwide loans also supplement the revolving displays. Female Buddhas and the comparisons of Western and Himalayan cosmologies are among topics addressed and considered. The museum also lends out a number of its exhibitions for travel to other venues.

Like most museums, *The Rubin* offers a number of programs, which in this case provides a great opportunity for cross-cultural awareness. Lectures, musical performances, discussions and film screenings are all utilized on *The Rubin's* calendar, to further spread the mission that Donald and Shelly Rubin envisioned. As for education, each of the museum's five floors contains an Explore Area, where computers offer an interactive look at the current subjects on display. There are also school and family learning programs available. The museum's location, near 14th street and its many subway outlets, makes *The Rubin* an easy place to get to, one worth exploring, as this museum presents such a unique and different tour.

The 1, 2, 3, 4, 5, 6, A, C, E, F, L, M, N, Q and R trains to their respective 14th Street stations all leave you within walking distance of *The Rubin Museum of Art*. The M5, M6, M7 and M20 buses all have stops on 18th Street and 6th or 7th Avenues, each a block from *The Rubin*.

- *MTA Today, New York City Transit Edition, 10/24/14*

___Walking Distance___*:* Union Square; Madison Square Park; Flatiron Building; National Arts Club; The Forbes Galleries; The Center for Jewish History; Theodore Roosevelt Birthplace.

Visiting the 9/11 Memorial--9/11 Memorial Museum

http://www.911memorial.org

On September 17, 2011, I had my chance to visit the *9/11 Memorial*, which had opened earlier that week, on the 10th anniversary of the attacks. Set-up amidst the loud and convoluted re-construction sites still in progress all around it, the *Memorial* is brilliant in its simplicity and powerful in its basic application. The two pools, which flow inside the footprints of the former North and South Towers, are surrounded on the base of those footprints by all the indented names of those lost on that darkest of days we now matter-of-factly call *9/11*. All those who died at the Trade Center, the Pentagon and the Pennsylvania countryside on September 11, 2001, as well as those who died in the February 26, 1993 basement truck bombing of the World Trade Center have their names stenciled into the perimeter of each Tower footprint, with North or South Pool coordinates (N-35, S-22, etc.) noted along the bottom rim of the footprints.

Kiosks located between the pools, against the still in-construction *9/11 Memorial Museum*, allow you to enter a name and find out exactly where that person's name could be found. For instance, a former Transit co-worker and friend, Denny Conley, was at S-65 and a great friend of mine from childhood, Sal Lopes, was at S-53. When you enter the *9/11 Memorial* after going through a maze of quick and efficient security (including an airport-like metal detector), the first thing you come upon is the South Pool, with the North Pool to your extreme left. The Museum, scheduled to open sometime in 2012 (though currently held up by funding issues), stands between the pools to the right, a long, odd, imposing structure which looks like a bent in half fallen building (artistic styling?). There is also an area to sit on concrete slabs nearer the North Pool. Large canvas guides posted against the outer fencing of the currently gated area tell you where different groups of victims are located (For instance, all of the first responders and the Pentagon victims are on the South Pool site; the February 1993 victims on the North Pool site.) The *Freedom Tower*, which will be the next celebrated tall building in Manhattan, hovers over the North Pool, looking rather mundane as it creeps higher to the once smoke-filled sky.

A visit to the *9/11 Memorial* is something I'd recommend to anyone, New Yorker or not, as a must see. I was both drained and inspired on my initial visit there and on subsequent visits in October and on my birthday in February of 2012 with good friends and co-workers Monah Johnson, Paula Alleyne and Asya Muid, they each offered up similar sentiments.

....

In May of 2014, the long awaited *9/11 Memorial Museum* opened at the former site of the World Trade Center, to complement the memorial pools that stand on the footsteps of the former North and South Towers. Gut-wrenching, thought-provoking and visceral, the *9/11 Museum* was, as one might expect, one of the most emotionally-charged venues you may ever see in your life. As a lifetime New Yorker, I applaud the efforts of those who conceived it, made it happen and richly honored the memory of all those lost on September 11, 2001.

The main exhibition space is located seven floors beneath the ground, or at the heart of the foundation of the Twin Towers. The "slurry wall" which kept the huge edifices firm and safe from the nearby Hudson River, is a remarkable item to view up close and the two huge surviving Tridents from the Plaza Level of the WTC, which one encounters upon entering the museum, remind all of the unique architecture of the buildings.

There are two main exhibits in the *9/11 Memorial Museum*. The historical *September 11, 2001* timeline exhibit, which lies beneath the North Tower footprint, gives an almost exhausting account of events that led to that previously unimaginable day, that Tuesday itself and the aftermath of the tragedy. The bravery of not only the fire, police, transit and EMS teams, but of everyday citizens who found themselves at the midst of an unprecedented nightmare are well documented. Personal items, various videos of the day and (audio) tapes made by survivors, interspersed with cell phone calls from victims, have a powerful impact on the visitor. The attack on the Pentagon and the bravery of passengers who forced the crash of Flight 93 into the Pennsylvania countryside, as well as the 1993 WTC truck bombing, are also properly represented.

The *In Memoriam* exhibit, located under the footprint of the South Tower, includes photos of all those lost in both Twin Towers' attacks. Kiosks on the floor of this area allow you to touch any victim's photo to view a profile of that individual. That particular application actually gave me a moment of joy; as I looked over profiles of my childhood friend, Sal Lopes, former co-workers Denny Conley and Luda Ksido and firefighter Leon Smith, Jr. (the son of retired friend and co-worker Irene Smith), I thought that it was a good thing that anyone could come here and get a small taste of who these people were in life and not just photos on a memorial wall.

The E train to the World Trade Center stop, the 4 or 5 to Fulton Street and the R to Rector Street all leave you within walking distance of the Liberty Street/Greenwich Street intersection, where the entrance to the entire *9/11 Memorial* rests.

- *MTA Today, New York City Transit Edition, Memorial, 6/5/13; Museum, 8/15/14*

Walking Distance: Trinity Church; Canyon of Heroes; Irish Hunger Memorial; The Anne Frank Center USA

Whitney Museum of American Art

http://whitney.org

One of the finer contemporary art museums you'll find anywhere is the *Whitney Museum of American Art*, located on 75th Street and Madison Avenue. At *The Whitney*, American art of all kinds from the 20th and 21st Centuries is celebrated and exhibited throughout its five floors. The work of living artists is particularly emphasized, while a large collection of works from the first part of the 20th Century graces the museum's archives.

Founder Gertrude Vanderbilt Whitney was a well-known sculptor and art collector. In 1918, she created the *Whitney Studio Club*, an exhibition space in New York City which promoted avant-garde and otherwise unknown artists. In 1929, when her offer to donate over 700 pieces of American art to the *Metropolitan Museum of Art* was declined and the new *Museum of Modern Art (MoMA)* showed a preference for European-based art, Whitney decided to create her own museum, for displaying exclusively American art.

In 1931, *The Whitney* was first established in three row houses on West 8th Street in Greenwich Village, one of which had been the home of her *Studio Club*. Whitney's assistant, Juliana Force, became the director of the museum and began the tradition of displaying the works of new and contemporary American artists. In 1954, *The Whitney* moved to a small space behind the *MoMA*. A fire on the second floor of the *MoMA* in 1958 forced some of their staff members and paintings to be relocated to *The Whitney*. In 1966, *The Whitney* moved to its current site. A new building is currently being designed and will open in 2015, between the High Line and the Hudson River.

Going to *The Whitney* recently, I saw a few really fine exhibits. *Blues for Smoke* showed the effect that blues music has had on live art. I went on the final weekend of that exhibit and I didn't see any of the live performances that were part of the display's run, but what I did see was very inspiring. *Jay DeFeo; A Retrospective*, which runs through June 2nd, highlighted one particular artist, while American

Legends; From Calder to O'Keeffe, a continuous exhibit, showed works from various artists, as did *I, You, We*, a collection of pieces from the 1980's and early 90's which had just opened on April 25th. One thing you can be sure of is that *The Whitney* always has a unique view of American art on display.

The *Whitney Museum of American Art* closed down its longtime home in late 2014, as they began moving all their assets to the new home at 99 Gansevoort Street, slated to open in the Spring of 2015. The A, C, E and L trains to 14th Street will leave you within walking distance of the new *Whitney*. The M11 and M12 buses will also have stops near the new *Whitney*.

- *MTA Today, New York City Transit Edition, 6/5/13*

Walking Distance: High Line; Chelsea Market.

(3)

Books

A few of my books which were featured on MTA Today;

See **authorhouse.com**

(Search: Thomas Porky McDonald)
to access these and other titles

Dem Poems: The Brooklyn Collection

In July of 1985, I arrived in Brooklyn to work for the New York City Transit Authority. For two decades, I surveyed the grounds, the air and the heartbeat of what I would come to consider my second home. More than anything though, I found the writer and poet within myself while navigating Brooklyn, and that translated into short stories, historical narratives and the poetry that defines this Irishman who showed up one day on the "G" train from nearby Queens.

Dem Poems: The Brooklyn Collection is a celebration of my 20 years spent as a Brooklyn regular, where some of the most relevant pieces in my arsenal were born. Beginning with a nod to the many fabled icons of the Borough, like the Brooklyn Bridge ("Steel Ropes"), Ebbets Field ("Bedford Interlude") and Coney Island ("Take a Message Back to Sundown"), as well as the area's landscape itself ("Just a Walk On Flatbush Avenue," "Trolley Tracks"), this volume then settles into more personal poems about those who first graced my life in Brooklyn. Pieces like "Notes On the Hallway Choir," "Sister Theresa" and "A Ride On the I.N.T." speak reverently of friendships shared and grown, while leading the reader toward the two most visceral sections in the collection.

Retirees ("Waltz into the Night"), escapees ("Southbound") and others moving on ("Bittersweet Moments") form a joyous prelude to a number of more somber homecoming pieces, such as "Sonic Whispers" and "Where Pain Doth Cease." In the final pages of the book, Brooklyn baseball, which was the original muse for me during my earliest days in Kings County, is lauded in both the past ("The Kids From the Old Neighborhood," "Dem, I and Eden," "The Sentry") and present ("At Brooklyn," "Eternity Day") forms.

This book is most significant to me, since it pays tribute to all of those friends and co-workers who influenced my writing and (especially) poetry for the two decades beginning in 1985, when I first came to Brooklyn on a permanent basis. In fact, the idea for this book came about one day when a great friend, Gail Dunmore, broached the idea of a Brooklyn poetry book, only hours after I had thought of the very same idea. The rest was easy, because the poems had already been written. And although Gail herself retired a few years later and thus did not make the *"Legacies"* section of **Dem Poems**, there is a piece in here I wrote for her when her mother passed away ("One More"), so I guess that rounds it all out. If you have been in Brooklyn as a Transit worker or otherwise for any significant time, this book may well be for you.

- *MTA Today, New York City Transit Edition, 7/26/12*

Diamond Reflections: Baseball Pieces for Real Fans

Taken from twenty-seven collections of poetry written between the years 1989 and 2006, ***Diamond Reflections: Baseball Pieces For Real Fans*** contains 291 poems about and fueled by the once and future National Pastime. Reflecting on a joyous childhood, my deep-rooted love for baseball, first instilled in me by my dad, Bill "The Chief" McDonald, flows vibrantly throughout this volume. As I'd done with previous chronological collections, I broke this book into three large sections, with a final piece to round it out.

In *Heroes*, personal favorites from a child of the late 60's-early 70's ("My Pal Willie," "Able to Find Cleon," "A Single Classic Swing") meld seamlessly with historical figures ("When the Man Came On Waving His Wand," "Me and the Splinter," "Waiting For Jackie Robinson") latter-day luminaries ("Safe Harbor," "San Diego's Pride") and often forgotten stars of the Negro Leagues ("Ol' Satch," "Mule in the Sky," "Thinking About Josh"). In *Playing Fields*, this formula continues, with the old ("The Park That Isn't There," "A Church I Never Went To," "Across Dimensions," "Merely Sunny Yesterday"), the new ("Outskirts," "Rockin' By the Lakeside," "Stillwell, Surf to Shore") and the personal memories of childhood ("The Peaceful Joy We Had," "Faith Between the Lines," "The Fields of the Lost, Scattered Youths," "Queensbridge") each checking in. In *Lessons*, personal beliefs and feelings inspired by or corroborated by baseball round out the collection. The most evocative of these include "A Big Small Town Known as Childhood," "Rainbows in Need of a Storm," "The Boy from Down the Hall," "Wooden Bats" and "When We Were All Poets." *A Final Tour*, whose singular piece, "Farewell to a Season," may most properly define the scope of the work (".... Laughter every inning, here to the beginning; Reach out youngster aging for the light."), closes out what I feel is both a personal and universal volume of poetry.

Inspired by the long ago work of Grantland Rice, I found myself, as an adult, still most at home at the ballpark, which brings me back

137

to (among others) childhood friends ("Faith Between the Lines") my maternal grandfather ("Ellwood Would Have Loved It") and my dad ("A Lefty Catcher," "Just We Two").

Diamond Reflections: Baseball Pieces for Real Fans is a unique collection in that so many baseball-themed verses are rarely found in one place. I am currently working on a second (smaller) volume of baseball-themed poetry called ***Seams So Eventful: More Baseball Pieces for Real Fans***, which will cover poems I've written from 2006 to the present. I think anyone who loves baseball will identify with many of the pieces in either of these collections.

- ***MTA Today, New York City Transit Edition, 6/14/13***

Irishman's Tribute Series

In 1971, when I was 10 years old, legendary pitcher Satchel Paige became the first player from the Negro Leagues to be voted into the National Baseball Hall of Fame in Cooperstown, New York. Having been brought up on baseball from about age 4 by my dad, William E. "The Chief" McDonald, this particular item spawned some new questions. After going over it with dad thoroughly, I found out that in another time in the not too distant past, a number of All-Time greats that I was growing up watching, like Willie Mays, Hank Aaron and Willie McCovey, would not have been allowed to play in the Majors, simply due to their skin color. This revelation drew an extremely spirited reaction from me: ballplayers are ballplayers. Skin color? Are you kidding me? As a result, I began studying the Negro Leagues and all of those who had been barred from the Big Leagues for no good reason. Decades later, after I had begun writing poetry and subsequent books, the early knowledge I'd gained served me well.

In writing a book dedicated to the Negro Leagues, I wanted to do something unique, as I owned a number of books on the subject, by wonderful historians like John Holway and James A. Riley. From the dogged research and interviews with many old timers, Holway, Riley and others gave me a template to imagine and even understand to a small degree what the Negro League experience was like. My book, *An Irishman's Tribute to the Negro Leagues,* became an anthology volume of poetry, player profiles and short stories, seemingly by chance. I had written many of the poems I'd use and the profiles were realized using Riley's *The Biographical Encyclopedia of the Negro Baseball Leagues*. The 10 short stories came quickly enough and *An Irishman's Tribute to the Negro Leagues* became the first book that I would publish; it looks better to me now, for what it was/ is and for what it led to.

I was raised Catholic and though I am not a regular churchgoer, the concept of a "Holy Trinity" has certainly permeated my writing. Many of the poetry books I have written follow a three-section format and as for the "Irishman's Tribute," I quickly thought to write follow-up anthologies to my Negro League book (the father), one about the greatest player ever, Willie Mays (the son) and another about the place where Jackie Robinson broke the color barrier, Ebbets Field (the Holy Ghost), with new poems, stories and historical content in the mix. I believe that all three books, ***An Irishman's Tribute to the Negro Leagues***, ***Over the Shoulder and Plant on One: An Irishman's Tribute to Willie Mays*** and ***Hit Sign, Win Suit: An Irishman's Tribute to Ebbets Field***, offer a pretty good reading experience, whether one is a baseball fan or not.

- ***MTA Today, New York City Transit Edition, 3/28/14***

Poet in the Grandstand

I have been writing poetry books since 1989. In the past decade, I have published a number of chronological collections, as well as a few other volumes. My most notable topic has been baseball, which has been a love of mine since I was about 4 years old.

Through my latest book, *Poet in the Grandstand*, a chronicle of 21 years on the road (1990-2010) going to various ballparks, I believe I give a most unique twist to a preoccupation which I have witnessed growing amongst the masses in the past few decades. In the wake of the closings of classic old yards and the birth of the more entertainment and nostalgia driven open-air parks, many people seem to be making a few trips a year to see Major (and Minor) League ballparks.

From my first trip in 1990, to see the fabled home of the White Sox, Comiskey Park on Chicago's South side, to the 2010 opening of Minnesota's fabulous Target Field, this book became part travelogue and part poetic tribute to all the places that men and women have gone to over the years for a very personal sense of joy. As the years went by, I was clearly growing as a poet. The result was that I wrote more and more pieces in the later trips. Ultimately, I'd written a most interesting volume of not just ballparks, but Americana, as numerous attractions taken in during those ballpark weeks and weekends are also noted and/or dissected.

For 14 seasons, I went on my own. For seven more I was accompanied by my friend and NYC Transit co-worker, Adam Boneker. Our travels, highlighted by over 300 poems that are included in *Poet in the Grandstand*, can take the reader back to a simpler time or into the possibilities of the future. I believe *Poet in the Grandstand* has something for the baseball enthusiast, the lover of poetry, and the curious traveler.

Thomas Porky McDonald

To date, I have gone to 55 ballparks, including a few I had been to before beginning the two-decade road trip which would ultimately become the "Poet in the Grandstand Tour."

- ***MTA Today, New York City Transit Edition, 1/6/12***

Poetry Collections

During my almost three decades at New York City Transit, one of the finest things that happened to me was the discovery of the poet within myself, which I do not think would have come out quite so vibrantly as it did and has, without having arrived in Brooklyn to work in 1985. I started writing serious poems around 1989 and in the years to follow, I would be able to share much of my work due to the creation of the Poet Tree club, which was formed by Rebecca McFadden and Linda Davis, two very sweet ladies who have retired from Transit in the past few years, as well as Chris Knight, another dear Transit co-worker, who is still active. But even before that club began and then thrived, I had begun compiling my poems into books and then collections, as the numbers grew, to my utter delight.

I somehow came into the habit of writing small poem books that consisted of 60-70 poems, though the original five were only 50-60. These smaller collections were then incorporated into five-book collections, which I then published in the chronological order in which they were written. Like most poets, my pieces are about life and things that I see in general, though I have written a considerable amount of poems about baseball, a topic and a game that has always meant a lot to me, ever since my dad first took me to Shea Stadium in the late 1960's. Along with the chronological collections, I have produced two specialty volumes, *Diamond Reflections: Baseball Poems for Real Fans* and *Dem Poems: The Brooklyn Collection*, which celebrated baseball and my 20 years in Brooklyn, respectively.

As for the yearly collections, I currently have six volumes available. In order, they are: *Ground Pork: Poems 1989-1994; Downtown Revival: Poems 1994-1997; Closer to Rona: Poems 1997-1999; Still Chuckin': Poems 1999-2002; In the Cameo Shade: Poems 2002-2005*; and *Vespers at Sunset: Poems 2005-2007*. The first collection, *Ground Pork*, contains 284 poems, while all the rest have at least 306 pieces. You can almost chart my development and growth as a poet growing with each set, as far as I can see. In any case, I have received a great amount of support in the Transit community and I owe much of the success and acceptance of my work to many within Transit's ranks.

In addition to those previously mentioned, I also have two more collections which will be going to be published in the next year or so: *And These Thy Gifts: Poems 2007-2009* and *After the Dream: Poems 2009-2011.*

• **MTA Today, New York City Transit Edition, 9/26/14**

Still Walking

How Sandy Tore Us Together

A Piece written for MTA Today about those returning to work at NYC Transit following Hurricane Sandy

How Sandy Tore Us Together

http://new.mta.info

On Monday, November 5, 2012, many of the temporarily displaced citizens of 2 Broadway arrived at 130 Livingston Street in Downtown Brooklyn, to go to work for the first time since the devastating Hurricane Sandy swept through the East Coast, one week earlier.

Since many of those had also spent a number of years as tenants in the Brooklyn hub, there was an air of familiarity to the proceedings. As the two designated assignment rooms filled up with employees from various departments, the acknowledgments from one to another were truly remarkable. As each face crossed your path, a heightened sense of humanity and camaraderie seemed to fill the air.

The optimum phrase spoken became *"How did you make out?"* Everyone wanted to know how everyone else was doing. Was their home intact? Was their family fine? How badly had the vicious storm of a lifetime affected them? The question hung momentarily over and over that day, with each new interrogator anxious to hear some form of good news.

Most people were doing well, which is why they were there in Brooklyn. Of course, the people not there, those we would all think of as the day went on, spurred the second most verbalized query that morning, *"Did you see or hear from so-and-so?"* It seems we had all heard about someone whom we had worked with who had lost their home or had it suffer severe damage during the storm. And we all hurt because of it. So we clung to one another in a most unique way.

Folks you had seen nearly every day in the corridors and elevators of 2 Broadway and merely nodded to – like neighbors on the same street – were suddenly more friendly and caring, or so it seemed. And you yourself were more open and feeling than you had remembered in a long, long time. A shared and unprecedented nightmare, which affected so many in this region and had attempted to tear us apart, had instead brought us closer together. We were Transit workers; we were tri-state residents; we were human beings.

It felt like Jury Duty that first day, only with friends at a familiar courthouse. While we waited for assignments, we were more conscious of one another and more grateful to have each other to lean onto. Whether you had worked for Transit for just a short time or were halfway through your 28th year (as I was), you were reminded that the greatest thing about working in this organization is the people you meet along the way. Five November, Twenty Twelve brought that reality back home once more. Brooklyn, our spiritual home for decades, treated us not as orphans, but as returning family members, as if we were the Dodgers coming back. At least until our current home at 2 Broadway was ready to be re-populated.

- ***MTA Today, New York City Transit Edition, 12/5/12***

A Time

There was a time when I was certain
the wind would always blow my way;
There was a time I missed tomorrow
and didn't speak of yesterday;
There was a time for love and aging;
Each in their own way hiding out;
There was a time when hope was endless;
When we roared on, without a doubt;
There was a time to understand life
as merely what goes on right now;
There was a time for subtle nuance,
lying just beneath your brow;
There was a time I heard no voices
of those that were not here no more;
There was a time when I was fearless
and fully iron to the core;
There was a time for running forward,
without a backtrack in the mix;
There was a time we waxed oblivious;
When joy was everyday a fix;
When I think of all those who've trusted me
to keep those times so very clear;
Through the dreams and loyalty we shared,
I find that time, it still is here.